T0113966

QABALAH

Made Easy

❖ Also in the Made Easy series ❖

The Akashic Records

Animal Communication

Astrology

Chakras

Connecting with the Angels

Connecting with the Fairies

Crystals

Discovering Your Past Lives

Energy Healing

Feng Shui

Goddess Wisdom

Lucid Dreaming

Meditation

Mediumship

Mindfulness

NLP

Numerology

Reiki

Self-Hypnosis

Shamanism

Tantra

Tarot

Wicca

QABALAH

Made Easy

Discover Powerful Tools to Explore
Practical Magic and the
Tree of Life

David Wells

HAY HOUSE

Carlsbad, California • New York City
London • Sydney • New Delhi

Published in the United Kingdom by:
Hay House UK, Ltd., The Sixth Floor, Watson House,
54 Baker Street, London W1U 7BU
Tel: +44 (0)20 3927 7290; Fax: +44 (0)20 3927 7291; www.hayhouse.co.uk

Published in the United States of America by:
Hay House Inc., PO Box 5100, Carlsbad, CA 92018-5100
Tel: (1) 760 431 7695 or (800) 654 5126
Fax: (1) 760 431 6948 or (800) 650 5115; www.hayhouse.com

Published in Australia by:
Hay House Australia Ltd, 18/36 Ralph St, Alexandria NSW 2015
Tel: (61) 2 9669 4299; Fax: (61) 2 9669 4144; www.hayhouse.com.au

Published in India by:
Hay House Publishers India, Muskaan Complex, Plot No.3, B-2,
Vasant Kunj, New Delhi 110 070
Tel: (91) 11 4176 1620; Fax: (91) 11 4176 1630; www.hayhouse.co.in

Text © David Wells, 2017

The moral rights of the author have been asserted.

The information given in this book should not be treated as a substitute
for professional medical advice; always consult a medical practitioner. Any
use of information in this book is at the reader's discretion and risk. Neither
the author nor the publisher can be held responsible for any loss, claim
or damage arising out of the use, or misuse, of the suggestions made, the
failure to take medical advice or for any material on third-party websites.

This book was previously published under the title *Qabalah*
(*Hay House Basics* series); ISBN: 978-1-78180-803-0

A catalogue record for this book is available from the British Library.

ISBN: 978-1-4019-6901-1
Ebook ISBN: 978-1-78817-282-0

Interior images: Veronika By/shutterstock; interior
illustrations courtesy of the author

Printed in the United States of America

'Everything in the Universe, throughout all its kingdoms, is conscious: i.e., endowed with a consciousness of its own kind and on its own plane of perception.'

Helena Blavatsky, co-founder of the Theosophical Society

Contents

List of Exercises   ix

Acknowledgements   xi

Introduction   xiii

PART I: SYMBOLISM AND THE TREE OF LIFE

Chapter 1: The History of Qabalah   3

Chapter 2: Building the Tree of Life   7

Chapter 3: Universal Laws   29

Chapter 4: Spirit Guides on the Tree of Life   37

Chapter 5: Tarot and Planets   47

Chapter 6: Understanding the Astrology   57

Chapter 7: Rituals in Life and on the Tree of Life   63

PART II: THE SEPHIROTH

Chapter 8: Malkuth   77

Chapter 9: Yesod   101

Chapter 10: Hod   113

Chapter 11: Netzach   127

Chapter 12: Tiphareth   143

Chapter 13: Geburah   153

Chapter 14: Chesed   163

Chapter 15: Da'ath   177

Chapter 16: Binah   183

Chapter 17: Chokmah   193

Chapter 18: Kether   203

PART III: THE 22 PATHS

Chapter 19: Working with the Paths   217

So What Now?   229
Bibliography   231
About the Author   233

List of Exercises

This is me   xvi

Drawing the Tree   11

Asking your guides   43

Planetary influences   49

Listening to your subconscious   55

The Qabalistic Cross   66

Chakra workout   67

Archangel protection ritual   71

Elemental homework   87

The Malkuth temple   92

A Moon diary   106

The Temple of Yesod   108

Vision bored   117

The Temple of Hod   121

Expressing your inner Netzach   131

The Temple of Netzach   135

Vision of the personality triangle   140

The Temple of Tiphareth   149

Cutting the cord   158

The Temple of Geburah   159

Chesed awareness   168

The Temple of Chesed   170

Vision of the soul triangle   175

Leaping over Da'ath   180

Silence is golden   187

The Temple of Binah   189

The Temple of Chokmah   198

Building the Tree on your body   207

The light of Kether   209

Vision of the spiritual triangle   213

This is me!   214

Acknowledgements

Writing a book can be a solitary experience, but producing a book is far from it, and I know this one wouldn't have happened but for these lovely people!

From Hay House UK, my gratitude to Diane Hill, Director of International Sales and Operations, for championing the idea of adding Qabalah to the Basics series, Commissioning Editor Amy Kiberd for making it a reality and Lizzie Henry for her meticulous editing. And the wonderful team at Hay House, headed by Michelle Pilley, Publisher and Managing Director. I am eternally grateful.

But writing any book is also about those days when you're not feeling it and are just gazing at the stars, waiting for divine intervention or a magic elf to do the work for you. Sooner or later, one of those things happens. It happens quietly and it happens through the humour of a text, the laughter over a cup of berry tea and the unveiling of the nonsense of personality, and it happens through friends. So, Andrew Stark, Lee Fadden and Lisa Lister, thank you for being divine and intervening when I needed it most.

Introduction

'We must be absolutely firm in saying that no book ever has or will be written to 'teach' any reader Qabalistic Wisdom. Such is impossible not for lack of will but through lack of means.'

WILLIAM G. GRAY, *THE LADDER OF LIGHTS*

Welcome to Qabalah.

You will notice that I didn't say 'Welcome to *the* Qabalah', and there is a good reason for that, which is perfectly put in the quote above: I am not so sure the definitive Qabalah exists. When I was writing this book, there were many moments of clarity; dreams and meditations were full of communion with guides and angelic beings, and lessons and wisdom flowed from those incarnate too. But the message that was shouted the loudest was that it was 'Qabalah' and not '*the* Qabalah'.

Perhaps the 'the' could only ever be replaced, if at all, by 'your'? For the goal isn't just to understand Qabalah, it's to understand *yourself and the worlds you live in through Qabalah*.

Qabalah is a spoken tradition. It's a spiritual path and a body of magical knowledge and practices that have been passed down from one teacher to another.

What makes this path so special is that it pulsates with energies you can work with and have a very real experience of. The path is learned not just through information given, but through exploration taken and through experience.

The central organization system of Qabalah is The Tree of Life, represented by a beautiful symbol that holds incredibly powerful energy. It is made up of 10 spheres, called Sephira, and 22 pathways, each of which holds specific energies. They are states of being, and not necessarily destinations. Every Sephira has an experience or a way of working within it, a place to go for magical journeys.

On these journeys, down pathways to great disks of energy, the teachings of Qabalah are brought to life by the beings you meet along the way – archangels and fairy folk and the manifestation of every thought and feeling you have. We always anthropomorphize these things; to use and understand energy, we put shape, form and even order around that which is untouchable, that which is invisible, that which defies a full explanation: our relationship with the universe and its relationship to us.

My hope for this book is that it reminds you of the amazing being that you are, that it empowers you and that it holds you accountable for every word and deed on this Earth and beyond – because you *are* accountable. No excuses accepted – the responsibility for your own sovereign state is in your hands and yours alone. It is your thoughts and feelings that create the world you live in. But walking the paths of Qabalah will offer wisdom and experiences that will help raise you up to fully embrace your higher self and bring its full light to Earth.

For my part, I commit to 'teaching over preaching', to opening doors and letting you see what's beyond rather than telling you what's there, because what's there is different for everyone. And it's all done through simple rituals, meditations and safe practices that will enhance your visualizations and stir your soul's memories and perhaps leave you seeking more.

You will find familiarity in this book; many so-called 'new age' practices are an expanded version of one or more of the experiences on the Tree of Life. As each of the 10 spheres on the Tree has its own correspondences to gods, goddesses, crystals, incense, planets, Tarot and so much more, you will find it supports and helps you understand your own existing practices, enhancing them too, I have no doubt.

See this book as the guide it is, walking beside you and whispering in your ear. I cannot tell you what will happen along the way, because this is your journey and not mine, but I can tell you that it will astound you, help answer some questions and bring many more to the fore, and in undertaking this journey you'll uncover more about yourself than you could ever have imagined.

I was lucky enough to study Qabalah over years of classes and in a group, and to further my knowledge through self-study, astrology and past-life work, as well as through some amazing experiences, not all of them comfortable. But I have only furthered it, not completed it. I have never even considered that as an option in this lifetime. There is always, always something new to learn, and putting this book together has taught me just how true that is.

Don't rush through this book – there are no prizes for finishing first. In fact the opposite may be true. Take your time; this isn't a book just to be read, it's a book to be experienced, and your pace is more likely to be set by your own guides and higher self than anything or anyone else. Surrender to that and lose Earthly time constraints and pressures whenever you can – you're on universal time now.

This book will bring the lessons you need, and have asked for in sacred contracts, into your life – *physically* into your life. Are you ready?

Exercise: This is me

This is a very simple exercise, one you do at the start of this process and then again at the end.

❖ Write one page about yourself, today, who you are right now. You can make it about anything you want – what you look like, what you do for a living, your deepest desires, your spiritual journey to date... Just tell me who you are. Handwrite it in your journal if you have one (and you probably should) or, if you're writing electronically, print it and keep it somewhere safe.

Setting your intention

❖ Now, based on that, what do you want from Qabalah? What is your intention? What dream do you want to bring into manifestation?

Here is my intention from over two decades ago:

> *To teach Qabalah in any way I can to as many people as I can.*

I cannot stress enough (which is why I will keep on doing it) that *this is real*. The power of Qabalah and its ability to transform lives is *very, very real* and it must be treated as a potent force for change. Make it change for the good of others and yourself. This will work through the covenants you've already made with your higher self and with those guides, angels and universal beings waiting to help you.

Now, if you're ready to take the outer concept of the Tree of Life, its symbols and philosophies, and build your own inner Tree, which will enhance your awareness of the world you inhabit and those beyond, deepen your understanding of the angelic worlds and elementals, and allow you to see your place in it all and stand strongly rooted in your truth, come on in!

Part I

SYMBOLISM AND THE TREE OF LIFE

Chapter 1

The History of Qabalah

Perhaps it's fitting that the origins of Qabalah are steeped in mystery. Some say the Archangel Michael, or Gabriel, Ratziel or Metatron, gave it to humanity, some put ancient Egypt at the centre of its arrival, and some have Moses bringing it to the Children of Israel. Legends all? One might be the truth; all might be the truth.

Using the Tree as a symbol is for some a reference to the fall from grace of Adam and Eve. In this scenario, God himself gave the teachings to a host of angels, who passed them to Adam, who in turn passed them to his children as a way of returning to the Garden of Eden. There is much symbolism in that sentence and as you continue your journey it will become clearer. Such is the way of learning Qabalah.

So, Adam taught Seth, who taught Noah, who taught Abraham, and then the teachings were taken to Egypt, and Moses, who learned even more from Metatron. Moses then passed Qabalah to the elders of the tribes. David and Solomon, Daniel and Ezekiel all had visions, teachings and rituals appearing to come from Qabalah – or is that a retrospective fit?

Whatever the exact history, there is a path from one teacher to another, a spoken tradition that's learned through information given, exploration undertaken and experience gained, and these tales, or truths, extend into recent history, with many famous playwrights, architects, scientists and artists having their talents applauded and associated with Qabalah.

In a world that seeks more tangible evidence, perhaps the *Sepher ha Zohar*, or *Zohar*, helps narrow things down a bit. It's the earliest form of written Qabalah. There are, however, some questions concerning when it was produced and by whom. Allegedly it was written by Rabbi Simeon ben Yochai, who lived around AD 100–190 in Israel, but some say Moses de Leon wrote it, in 13th-century Spain, from Rabbi Simeon ben Yochai's teachings. Either way, the connection to Judaism is undeniable, but Qabalah is to be found in Christianity, Sufism and of course in western occultism too.

Its teachings moved through history, from the great Egyptian city of Alexandria, where many different spiritual teachers and philosophers met, debated and wove together a rich tapestry of vast wisdom, to France and Poland, gathering information from many sources along the way, and arriving in England in the late 19th and early 20th centuries.

Through the Hermetic Qabalah schools and the western esoteric tradition, the information was understood more, written about and worked with throughout the centuries. The Christian Church used it and so too did many other faiths and religions, as we have seen, but there is something very important to understand here: Qabalah does not seek to *divide*, it seeks to *provide* – provide a way to the highest realms of enlightenment through the experience of life and a connection to the spiritual worlds, whether you're a celebrity or not! The knowledge and wisdom are there to be used for the greater good.

The history of Qabalah is intricate; by its very nature, veils are drawn over it, though much is hidden in plain sight too. But, no matter how it got to you today, here it is.

Chapter 2

Building the Tree of Life

The Tree of Life in its very basic form is a symbol. It is a drawing that holds within it the very essence of the universe, but, like all symbols, it can't come alive until you breathe life into it. Consider a statue of your favourite spiritual icon, be it Buddha, Christ or Archangel Michael. The plaster, bronze or even golden statue is itself just a statue; it's the embodiment, the ensoulment of the energy that's been invested in the image that makes it so very special to you – to all of us.

For centuries, symbols have rallied nations. What is a flag but a symbol? Banners have separated and bound humanity and still do, so it's not such a surprise that the Tree of Life is a powerful symbol, considering it's had thousands of years of energy poured into making it so.

Symbols work on our subconscious mind; they bring many meanings, all wrapped up in one simple drawing, picture or icon, as well as a vibration of their very own, something that will become increasingly important as we go on. Think of that Buddha statue – what do you see when you look at it? What do you feel? How does it change you and what do you aspire to when you walk away from it? Does thinking of certain symbols help you to centre yourself, and if it does, do you do that often enough?

Now imagine a symbol that does everything the Buddha statue does but also points out where you are now and what you can do to help yourself if you want to change your location, and will also attract the right energy into your life to help you get there, all under the direction of your own will.

It also allows you to communicate with your angels, your guides, your Aunty Vera and your soul, as well as offers you information on how to deal with co-workers, what your life purpose is and just why you should avoid some situations and embrace the challenge of others. It's all things to all people, but above all, it's *your* Tree – no dogma, no 'have to', no 'follow me' or 'follow a religion'. It communicates through symbols – your symbols. Your own creative nature is your own Tree of Life.

Now think about negative symbols, things that draw you towards dour thoughts rather than positive ones, for they have just as much power. Removing them from your life is important – you don't need them. No matter how, when or why they've come to you, it's time to say bye-bye to those symbols that no longer serve you. Let them go with gratitude, with the understanding that they have brought you to where you are now, but let them go.

Start by switching off the news channel. Even the theme music to the news will prompt negativity, and if you watch death, destruction and argumentative politicians, your head will be full of those kind of thoughts and your angry response will overshadow the lightness of your spirit.

Don't mistake this for being in a world of your own, oblivious to what's going on around you – that's not what's being suggested. It's just that it's best to concentrate on yourself – your soul, your spirit and your link with the divine. Make your own choices.

There will be more challenges to come – they're unavoidable – but the Tree will highlight their lessons and show you the way through the toughest of times, just as it will help you make the best of the good ones.

What you will need

Begin by gathering the materials you will need for the journey. It's basic and fundamental to putting your spiritual development in order. Here's a list:

- A journal. You'll need to write down everything you experience, every symbol you see and every feeling; thought or sign that comes your way, for they will all be relevant. Use it as your dream book too. Record your dreams, as your subconscious will continue to give you information even when you're asleep, and it's likely to be more active than ever as you begin this journey.

- Next, a good symbol book. This will help you decipher the meaning of that dove, rose or lion that keeps popping up in your meditations. As you do this, you'll be building your own symbol store, which your subconscious will use to keep you on track. There's always the internet too, but go easy there – check and double-check the meanings given, and most of all check with your own gut instinct.

- A pack of Tarot cards – I use the Thoth deck – to help you understand the Tree and provide you with more information. Every card in the deck has its place on the Tree of Life – every one. If you haven't studied the Tarot, get a good book like Kim Arnold's *Tarot: Learn How to Read and Interpret the Cards* (*see Bibliography*). There's no need to learn the Tarot first – you'll learn more as you go along – but as you move through the Tree, it will help you understand it more. And if it does spark a bigger interest in the Tarot, there are many resources available to further your knowledge.

- The same goes for astrological influences on the Tree: you'll learn more about them as you go. That's something I really loved about my journey up the Tree – the wonderful mix of learning new things and the magic that runs through them all. If you would like to have a book on astrology for reference, a great one is *Parkers' Astrology* by Julia and Derek Parker.

Drawing the Tree of Life

No-thing

To get a better understanding of the Tree and begin to appreciate its structure, you are going to draw it, but before you begin, let's pause a moment to look at the three levels of being above the Tree: the Three Veils of Negative Existence.

- *Ain*, which means 'not' or 'nothing', 'no-thing', and is totally incomprehensible to us.

- *Ain Soph*, which means 'no limit, infinity'.

- *Ain Soph Aur*, which means 'limitless or infinite light'. This is slightly more tangible than the others, but still beyond our true understanding.

But consider this: whilst it's difficult for us to understand these veils, that doesn't mean they don't influence us. They do. They exert pressure. They give rise to our own Tree of Life. The universe, it's suggested, comes from the divine breath of God. I find that a wonderful description. The out-breath, that's the pressure perhaps? 'The breath taken before a word is spoken' describes these veils perfectly.

Perhaps whilst we're incarnate here on Earth this is as much as we need to know, and as a Qabalist of many years, I must confess these realms are outside my understanding and I start with Kether, the highest point on the Tree. Let's start drawing the Tree there.

Exercise: Drawing the Tree

- Get yourself a coin, maybe a dollar or a 10 pence piece.

- Take a blank sheet of A4 paper, find the centre vertically and draw a faint pencil line from top to bottom.

- Now find the midpoint between that line and the edge of the paper, on both the right and left-hand side, and draw vertical lines from those points so you have three lines on which to centre your circles and balance your Tree.

As you draw the Tree, what you're drawing and why will be briefly explained, and don't worry, more explanations will follow as we go along. You'll build on your knowledge piece by piece, adding layer upon layer, just like your Tree, and filling your symbol store with riches enough to last many lifetimes, as well as remembering those golden nuggets of information you've left already!

So let's begin. To help you, here's what you're aiming for.

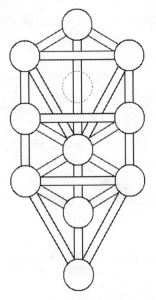

Figure 1: The Tree of Life

Don't panic, it's not as complicated as it looks, like so many things in life, and when you take your time and take one step then another, it will all make sense.

Each of the spheres is a Sephira; the plural is Sephiroth. See them as powerhouses of energy. They are states of being and will show themselves as conditions in your life and the lives of those around you. Pretty quickly they will become very familiar to you. It may even be more a case of remembering than learning.

To draw the Sephiroth:

❖ Take your coin and place it at the top of your paper. Centre it on your middle line and draw around it. This is Kether, where it all begins. Write the words 'Kether' and 'Crown' inside the circle and put the number one in there as well. Kether is where the divine in us and in the universe sits, waiting for the manifestation process to begin, holding onto every creative idea there is and ever will be until they are accessed – accessed and brought down.

❖ Now drop down to your right-hand side and draw another circle. Inside it write the words 'Chokmah' (pronounced *Hok-ma*, with the 'Ch' we Scots say in 'loch') and 'Wisdom' and the number two. Here those creative ideas are stimulated, charged with energy and hooked into the universal grid.

❖ Move across to the left-hand side of your page on the same level as Chokmah and draw your next circle. It's called Binah (*Bee-na*). In it, write the word 'Understanding' and the number three. It's here that those ideas are first given form, structure and direction.

❖ Now move back to the right-hand side under Chokmah and draw circle number four, Chesed (*Hess-ed*) and write 'Mercy' in it and the number four. As you do so, consider what excites you in life, where you practise generosity, what opportunities come to you when ideas flow and how you can sometimes get carried away with it all.

❖ Then it's back to the left with the next circle, Geburah (*G-boo-rah*). Here, write the word 'Severity' and the number five. Here is where you edit, make changes and cut away the excess as you realize that some things aren't necessary or even desirable.

❖ Into the centre now as you draw Tiphareth (*Tiff-a-reth*) and write the word 'Beauty' and the number six. If you look at this circle, you will see it sits at the centre of the Tree. It's about balance and finding the beauty in that moment of balance.

❖ Back to the right and Netzach appears (*Net-sack*). Write in the word 'Victory' and the number seven. Here's where you acknowledge your feelings. For the first time on this journey things get personal and seem to relate to day-to-day stuff more.

❖ Then over to Hod, the word 'Splendour' and the number eight. Your thoughts are represented here. This is where you create images, and be they negative or positive, you have the power to change your attitude, no matter what's going on around you, by changing your mindset.

❖ Then it's back to the centre and Yesod, the word 'Foundation' and the number nine. Here is where you store all your emotions, your memories and your past-life conditioning, and where you can get lost in repeating cycles.

❖ Finally, the last Sephira, Malkuth (*Mal-cooth*). Write in the word 'Kingdom' and the number 10. Take a look around you, for here you are, on Earth. You currently live in Malkuth. Is it the end point or is it the beginning?

(*You can download blank Trees of Life on my website: davidwells.co.uk/ qabalah.*)

Looking at your Tree so far, you will see that what is simply 10 circles on a page is already beginning to make more sense. By attaching words to the symbols you have drawn, you start to imbue them with magical energy, and that in turn brings the attention of universal energies your way, as they recognize the efforts you're making and the light you're switching on.

Da'ath

You will have noticed that just below Kether, between Binah and Chokmah, there is a dotted circle. This is called Da'ath, the great Abyss. It will be discussed later, but for now write the word 'Knowledge' in there.

'Which end is up again?'

Some folks get a little confused about to how to use the Tree in situations that are very personal and perhaps those that are environmental. It's all a question of perspective.

If you're looking at the Tree square on, as you're doing from the pages of this book, you're looking at the universal Tree, a Tree that's about the world(s) you live in and how that environment affects you: the macrocosm. If you imagine sitting with the Tree behind you, the middle pillar on your spine, this is your personal Tree: the microcosm.

Yes, that does mean that as you sit with the Tree at your back what's on your right as you look at it is now on your left, but your perspective is fundamental to working with the Tree. It all depends on the issue. If it's personal, you will put your spine on the Tree; if it's universal, you will face it.

Lightning flash

Going back for moment to the way you drew the Sephiroth, as you follow the energy down, you will notice it takes this direction:

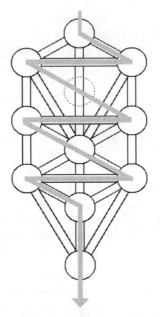

Figure 2: Energy flow through the Tree

If you follow the energy through, you can begin to see how the process of manifestation works. This works for anything from your own soul's incarnation right through to baking a batch of cupcakes, and knowing more means taking more control of the process so that you get that recipe just right.

Colours

Go back over your drawing and this time colour the Sephiroth in: colour my Qabalah! Each of the Sephiroth has a particular colour associated with it (*see below*). Colour is the first language of symbolism. Think about what the colour you're using says to you.

- *Kether:* An idea is waiting to be recognized and grabbed. Bright white with flashes of electric blue – truth and purity.

- *Chokmah:* It's charged with the spark of creativity. Grey, neither black nor white – a range of possibilities.

- *Binah:* Structure is put around it and it is given form. Black as night – deep meditation, form.

- *Chesed:* Excitement builds, ideas flow, opportunities exist. Royal blue – luxuriousness, spirituality, richness, peace.

- *Geburah:* Anything unnecessary is removed. Red, ruby red – being assertive, active, sensual; karma.

- *Tiphareth:* The idea is balanced and its true beauty shines. Yellow – golden days, creativity, the Sun.

- *Netzach:* Time to invest your feelings and joy into it. Emerald green – nature's colour, fertility.

- *Hod:* Time to brand and create the image. Orange – thoughtfulness.

- *Yesod:* Remember old pitfalls and learn from the past. Silver and purple mixed – memories, the Moon.

- *Malkuth:* Time to land. Russet, ochre, olive, brown – the colours of Earth.

The four worlds

Qabalah states that we exist in four worlds – not four planets, but four aspects of the divine, the divine within us and external to us. Each of us has a way of being in and being of these worlds.

Atziluth

Atziluth means 'Stand near' and this is where all that is willed into being waits, literally stands near, for the moment it can begin to realize its potential. Your divine spark is here; this world is where you come from and where you will return to. You will see in the following diagram it holds only one Sephira, Kether. That always feels like a reminder that the source of all things operates from Kether in utter purity, creating the Tree you're about to experience.

In Tarot this world is where the four knights/kings sit. Its element is Fire.

Briah

The spiritual world manifests through the 10 mighty archangels, whose names you will come to know as you progress through the Sephiroth. Expansion, contraction and balance are important here to help manifest peace within you. Here are the teaching rooms, the schools and divine temples of the inner planes, where your immortal self gathers information as well as informs the universe, God, of what you have learned and have still to understand. Here is the mighty Archangel Metatron, the great headmaster, gatherer and keeper of information.

The Tarot association here is with the four queens and the element is Air.

Yetzirah

Here are the astral worlds, where images are formed before manifestation in dreams, visions and meditation. Here we meet the hosts of angelic beings responsible for the world we see in front us, from the stars in the firmament to the blade of grass under our feet. Here, too, we meet disincarnate humans, living in their version of heaven, or not, of their own choosing. Our emotional body is often considered to be here too, in a dimension that's the final halt before the physical.

The four princes/knights of the Tarot sit here, as well as the element of Water.

Assiah

The final world, Assiah, is unsurprisingly the physical world, where we experience our incarnate existence. It's the densest of all four worlds and as such has rules attached, universal laws. We will discuss these later.

The Tarot cards are the four princesses/pages and the element is Earth.

In each sphere of Qabalah, the energy, the vibration, slows down, and as it passes from the world of the divine through the spiritual and astral worlds and into the physical world, it becomes denser and denser. This is the connection between human and God, source, divine energy – whatever you choose to call the expression of all there is.

It's important to remember the worlds are connected. They don't work individually, they work as one, as you are already one with the Godhead, energy or source.

Just to add a little more to your thought process on these worlds, imagine in each world there is another Tree. It helps to consider the integrations of all four worlds within you, so Kether exists not only in Atziluth but also in Briah, Yetzirah and Assiah.

The Sephirothic Triads

If you look at your Tree, you will see it can be split into three triangles:

- *The Supernal Triad:* Binah, Chokmah and Kether. This governs the bigger picture, humanity as a whole, and can be seen as your spiritual triangle.

- *The Etheric Triad:* Tiphareth, Geburah and Chesed. This is about your intuition and your soul, as well as the soul of humanity, and is seen as your soul triangle.

- *The Astral Triad:* Yesod, Hod and Netzach. This one is personality led and of course reflects not just your own personality but that of humanity too. So it is seen as your personality triangle.

Malkuth, home sweet home, is at the bottom waiting to receive all this information.

You will also notice that the bottom two triangles point down, the top up, suggesting the direction of their focus perhaps. The higher Sephiroth pointing up, the lower down – consider that for a moment.

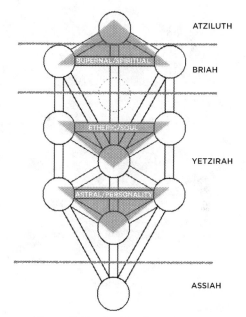

Figure 3: The Sephirothic Triads

The three pillars

Now it's time to consider the other structures that help bring the Tree to life. First the pillars. These are easy to see when you look at your drawing. There are three:

- one on the left, containing Binah, Geburah and Hod, known as the Pillar of Severity

- one in the centre, holding Kether, Tiphareth, Yesod and Malkuth, known as the Middle Pillar

- one on the right, with Chokmah, Chesed and Netzach, known as the Pillar of Mercy

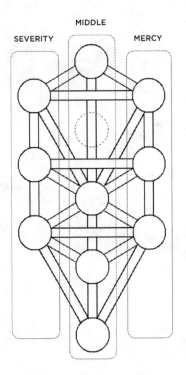

Figure 4: The three pillars

Now let's consider each in turn.

The Pillar of Severity

Binah

This is the Great Mother, directing with an understanding that goes beyond what might be obvious to those who are on the receiving end of her decisions. She shows you where you might experience limits, but limits that will ultimately shape your destiny. This Sephira of silence takes those difficult decisions.

Geburah

Often this Sephira is seen as challenging, but all it really wants to do is to cut away what is no longer required. Sometimes its influence is felt through trials and tribulations, but if you recognize that what's truly happening is losing what's not necessary, aren't you better equipped to deal with it? This will turn what you may have perceived as a weakness into a strength.

Hod

This is concerned with worldly matters like business and career, with how you approach these things, how you communicate and what images you create. It asks, 'How do you think – with your head, your heart, your gut?' It is an absolute powerhouse of affirmations, as you seek to create your world through positive thoughts and images.

The Pillar of Mercy

Chokmah

The opposite number to the Great Mother! Here you will find the Cosmic Father, balanced behaviour and responsibilities. Logic is the way of Chokmah, but don't think of this as a dull Sephira – it's very far from it. When choices need to be made that require both logic and sudden illumination, this is the place to be!

Chesed

Here you're rewarded for the work you've put in, the opportunities you've been prepared to take and the adventurous side of your nature that has helped you take them. Compassion, peace and positivity are reflected in Chesed, and here you can manifest abundance, be that spiritual, financial or emotional.

Netzach

Your feelings and emotional attachments are represented here – what you desire and perhaps who you find attractive as well as who your BFF is and what makes them that. Use Netzach to understand your relationships, what you want from them and how others make you feel when you're around them.

The Middle Pillar

Kether

At the crown of the Tree of Life sit your full potential, new starts and inspirational ideas. Here are the spiritual realms and that place you go to when you're sitting on your rug, eyes closed and no-thing bothering you. But it can also be where you lose yourself and become so heavenly-minded that you're no Earthly good.

Tiphareth

A beautiful Sephira, which represents your higher self, or maybe what is best described as your soul. It's all about higher ideals as well as where you meet that part of yourself that would sacrifice all for those you love. It sits at the centre of the Tree and therefore at your own centre too. Can you remember the last time you felt truly balanced?

Yesod

Habits and cycles are shown here – what you repeat. When you know how to look into the mirror of this Sephira, you will be able to see where those habits or patterns come from – this life, past lives...? This Sephira also shines a light on your hopes and fears as well as affecting your physical dreams and allowing the subconscious to communicate clearly. The question is, do you want to listen?

Malkuth

Your kingdom on Earth, the physical world you live in. All that's manifest in your life is here. Here you become consciously aware of everything above you, to your left and to your right. All you have done gathers in Malkuth, including in your physical body, which is the vehicle for all your thoughts, feelings, dreams, aspirations, logical decisions, adventures, tough love, images... You get the picture.

So, in brief, the three pillars are:

- *Severity:* Here are found the principles of taking tough decisions when they need to be taken, in a way that is firm but fair. What needs to be done in order to move towards your goal. Divine justice.

- *Mercy:* Here is your benevolent side, the part of you that wants peace and, when you have brought it into your life, to enjoy that peace and all the rewards of your efforts. Divine mercy.

- *Middle:* When you have cut away what doesn't work and embraced all those opportunities that have come your way, you will find yourself in a place of balance. Divine!

Now consider where these pillars sit on your body. If you have your back to the Tree, your right side is Severity, your left is Mercy and clearly the Middle goes down your spine.

Consider your physicality in terms of the Tree. Could there be a problem in the spiritual realm that's manifesting in the physical? If you're experiencing pain on your left-hand side, are you being too generous, giving too much to others? If you're a healer, this could give another dimension to your work.

That also brings into consideration where the Sephiroth sit on the human body.

The Tree on your body

From this diagram you'll see where the Sephiroth sit on your body, and if you're involved in energy work, you'll see how they correspond to the chakra system. More of that later. For now, think about where they sit on your body and what that could tell you about a pain or an odd sensation around a particular area. I'm not for one second suggesting that as a substitute for professional medical advice, but as you work with the Tree you may feel the Sephiroth physically, some people do, and I would hate you to miss out on any information the Tree can impart.

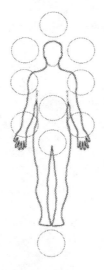

Figure 5: Where the Sephiroth sit on your body

So:

- *Kether* is above the head
- *Chokmah* on the left side of your face
- *Binah* to the right
- *Da'ath* not shown, but on your throat
- *Chesed* your left arm and shoulder
- *Geburah* your right arm and shoulder
- *Tiphareth* your solar plexus
- *Netzach* your left hip and leg
- *Hod* your right hip and leg
- *Yesod* your genitals
- *Malkuth* your feet

If you want to take this information further, you might consider the significance of a constant pain, or a returning injury or sensation. Where is it? As you move through the Sephiroth, it may be highlighted again. As you find out more about each of these powerhouses, be aware of what your body could be telling you. If you are aware, you can fix it!

Remember the four worlds of Atziluth, Briah, Yetzirah and Assiah? What if the energy from an issue in Yetzirah was being mirrored in Assiah, reflected in your physical body?

Just as your body mirrors the Sephiroth, they can be seen working in the world around you through the laws of the universe. Let's stop and consider them. You'll be familiar with some of them already, but referring back to the Tree of Life will help bring clarity and recognition – it opens your mind and heart to what's really going on!

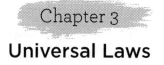

Chapter 3

Universal Laws

To better understand how you might see the influence of the Sephiroth in your life, or how you might use them perhaps, you need to know these undeniable laws. They can help put events and situations into the context of the Tree of Life, and that will hopefully help you find your way out of those you don't want or attract more or those you do!

Kether

No. 1: The law of expression or creativity

Creativity. It's something we admire in others. How often do we say, 'I wish I was more creative'? You can hear yourself saying it, I'm sure! Do you know that you're just as creative as the next person, it's just that you may not have taken the time to find how to express it yet?

Creativity is an expression of who you are. At its very heart, it's simply being yourself, bringing yourself to a project or a situation. You don't have to compare yourself to anyone else or copy anyone else. It's easy to just do the bidding of your boss or of someone who is bossy, but is that what you've incarnated for?

Think of the Sephira that's associated with this law. Think of the moment where no-thing exists, so no-thing is impossible. From that point, what would you choose to make possible?

Create something for itself and for no other reason. Start something new in your life because it seems like fun and make it an expression of yourself.

Chokmah

No. 2: The law of rotation or cycles

We all know that life moves in cycles, the obvious ones being the seasons and the rising and setting of the Sun. You can see cycles in fashion, in governments and in your own moods. As the great wheel turns, recognize what cycle you're in, where you are in it and how you can use it to make your life easier.

Most likely you already do, but where? Can you think of a cycle you adhere to? If you have children, you'll know that every year at a certain time there's book week, then there's the Halloween party and so on, and you can be ready for it or not!

Some cycles you can't change, like the seasons, for example. You'll also see cycles in those you love – when they are more vibrant, when they slow down – and you may not be able to change those either. The move from birth to death is a cycle too. Whether we like it or not, the wheel turns.

Where do you need to be more patient and wait for the right moment rather than ignore the cycles you see?

Binah

No. 3: The law of polarity

Polarities: there are male and female, hot and cold, dark and light, yin and yang, and you probably have more to add to the list. Polarities are all around us, but they should complement each other, with neither being dominant, and if things do move out of synch they should compensate quickly.

In your own life this may mean using the power of silence to allow time for someone to restore their own balance, or could it be about putting form around the chaos they have going on in their life by using what they're missing but you have in abundance? If one person is great at accounts and the other superb with customers, it makes for a good business, but what if neither is that great with customers?

Can you identify a situation where you are yin to someone else's yang? Or where more hot is needed to balance the cold?

Chesed

No. 4: The law of order and timing

Isn't that the same as cycles? Not quite. Perhaps it's best described as being linear rather than circular.

The law of order and timing is knowing that everything has its time and place. The flower grows and at the perfect time it will bloom. It's also about the order and timing of your soul choices, about listening to what is your true will and living it rather than falling into the trap of hypocrisy or, worse still, bigotry.

In your own life it's knowing enough to let things go with the energy of the moment, but also knowing when it's time to do your bit. Taking that flower, for example, it may know it's time to bloom and do it beautifully, but the bee that visits the bloom also knows it's time to get some pollen for honey, which in turn pollinates the flower. Sometimes you just need to *be* before you can blossom.

Look at a project in your life. Truly observe it and know whether you need to be involved in it now or not.

Geburah

No. 5: The law of cause and effect

This is one of those laws that really needs no introduction! Look at the Sephira it's associated with!

The law of cause and effect is quite simple: for every action, there is an equal and opposite reaction. Another way of looking at it is karma. You'll see this clearly in your own life, without even needing to delve into past lives. Your actions have consequences.

Sometimes you know what could come back at you and yet you feel so passionately about something, you just have to go with it anyway. But there are limits. Cause and effect can adjust and bring change, but must never, ever, be allowed to move into cruelty, where you just don't care what damage you cause.

Can you see where cause and effect could work really well for you in your life? We often look at the negative connotations of this law, but think of the positive. Through giving time or money to charity work, for example, we bring about far-reaching change. Look at your own life. Where can you bring in more of the positive by doing more of the positive?

Tiphareth

No. 6: The law of adaption or change

We adapt. It's what we do. But is adaption change, pure and simple? Could it be a warning too? If you lost a limb, you would adapt to make the most of what you had left. What if you were kept prisoner? Would you adapt and make the most of that? Would you adapt to bigger jeans instead of looking at the cause and effect of eating too many doughnuts?

Don't adapt negatively, adapt positively. Adapt upwards – adapt and change as you devote yourself to a greater cause or commitment. Raise your vibrations and use the law of adaption positively by spending time with those who do that for you naturally. Tribes and vibes. Where can you adapt purposely? Where can you invite change in?

Netzach

No. 7: The law of relativity and perception

Some weeks pass quickly, some seem to drag. Perhaps that's relative to what you're doing or how you perceive the time that you have. If you're on holiday, time passes all too quickly. If you're doing a boring job, it slows down, bringing you long hours filled with mind-numbing tasks!

Perception can also be a tricky thing. Acting on what you see means acting on what you see from *your* angle. Change that perspective and you might see something totally different. You might think someone is a right royal pain; what you might not know is why they're behaving that way. That child making too much noise while their parent pays no attention whatsoever – annoying, isn't it? Until you find out the parent has just taken a phone call with some devastating news in it and is in a state of shock.

What's really going on in your life? What could you be seeing from just one angle? Where do you need to find out that little bit more about a situation? And time – what if there were no time? Let things unfold!

Hod

No. 8: The law of images

I subscribe to the idea that thoughts aren't ours, they float on past us and we feel them, see them, experience them, however we do it. But do we always *act* on them?

If you have an idea for a great invention and a few years later there it is, someone else has made it happen. Have they read your mind or just taken the idea that was floating about and done something with it?

An idea that floats past is one image you might have in your head. What you build in your mind is, however, different. If you keep thinking the same thing over and over again, it will manifest. Negative or positive, it doesn't matter. So, keep the images, and the chat, inner and outer, as positive as you can. Always. Catch yourself saying something negative about yourself and *stop right there*. I don't just mean stop doing it, but stop and consider how it's making you feel. Now change it. How does that make you feel?

Yesod

No. 9: The law of reflection

We all know that when we meet someone we like, we mirror their actions. It's basic body language – they cross their arms, we do it; they play with their drink, we do it.

Take that a step further and you see life reflecting back messages all the time, through songs, television programmes, books, other people... Look, there you are – situations in other people's lives that are in yours too!

Recognize this process. Then detach from your emotional reactions to it. Find a way to use what you see without letting it take you on an even deeper journey into the emotions of it all. Step back and consider what it's telling you.

Be aware of those prompts, those moments that tell you not only what needs to change but also what you may need more of in your life.

Malkuth

No. 10: The law of discrimination and action

What do you really need to do right now? If you have to make a pie, you can't fill it before you've made the pastry, but first you have to decide to make the pie and actually do it! Does the pie have to be made before the potatoes are done? Probably, so you do that first, don't you? Or maybe you don't want a pie, you want a takeaway... Do it, don't do it, either way, but make a decision and act on it or you'll remain in the land of doing nothing, the land of inertia.

Here on Earth, nothing happens without action – fact. Is there something you want to see happen? You can think it, dream it, see it, feel it, ask your angels about it and/or get a crystal glowing, but nothing will happen until you decide where it lies on your list of priorities and then get on and do something about it.

Where have you been leaving an event, an action, up to a higher power without participating in it yourself?

Chapter 4

Spirit Guides on the Tree of Life

We all need a little help from time to time and there are many teachers out there, and not all are Earthbound. When you feel a little lost and are wondering which direction to go in, you might like to contact your spirit guides.

Spirit guides

There are several realms of spirit guides and they act in different ways, but with all guides, remember to ask for their help; they cannot act directly unless you ask. You will have plenty of opportunities to commune with them in the next few chapters.

Spiritual guidance can sometimes be a little difficult to spot, but it gets easier with time, and easier still when you receive that guidance in meditation and through the workings of the Tree of Life.

Earthly guides: Malkuth

Having said that, not all guides are that hard to spot. The first realm of guides is very easy in fact: they are your family and friends. Found right in front of you in Malkuth, yoo-hoo, there they are, helping guide you, and in particular helping guide you with choices you make on Earth, in the physical world.

These guides are more than capable of advising you on important matters from their soul rather than their personality. You will find people usually do that when it's truly important stuff. Don't forget to ask, though, as they will ask you. Of course they will have shared past lives with you, of course they are likely to have signed up to help you, and you to help them – they are all spiritual beings, just like you, spiritual beings having a human experience.

This brings to mind a very obvious observation: you are and have been a spirit guide, not always incarnate, but also working on an astral level.

Lifetime guide: Yesod

Next on the list is your lifetime guide. Notice the singular here – there's only one of them and they were with you at the moment you were born and will be with you when you shake off this mortal coil. They are usually someone with a past-life interest who knows you very well indeed. They know the true you, the inner workings of your soul, why you have incarnated and the lessons you want to get from this journey.

So, your lifetime guide has an overall picture. Like all guides, they can't directly influence you, but they can put suggestions and ideas to you, and, as they often work through Yesod, these can come in images projected from Hod, where the Akashic Records, the past-life library, and the book containing your soul's journey are housed. It's whether or not you want to take these suggestions, or even notice them, that's the challenge.

Sometimes people see their grandma or another person who has crossed over as a guide. This won't be a lifetime guide, unless they crossed before you were born perhaps, but a personality guide, who helps with personal stuff. If they are around, they too will reside in Yesod, as it's the home of the astral worlds.

Doorkeeper: Yesod

Your doorkeeper is also to be found in Yesod. Doorkeepers are protectors. In particular, they stand in front of you to keep your crown chakra safe during spiritual travels, making sure you close down between your meditations and your Earthly return. By that I simply mean they won't let any negative energy affect you as long as you keep yourself under some sort of control. They don't work very well if you are under the influence of drugs or alcohol, which isn't any judgement on those who use them to excess, it's just telling it how it is.

These massive beings are often scary in appearance. They present themselves as warriors. They can be either male or female, but being fierce in appearance is part of the deal. When I first met mine it was quite a shock!

Teacher guides: Hod and Netzach

Teacher guides move in and out of your life. They may stay with you for a month or a decade, but their influence is very strong and they have definite ideas about getting you to see your potential. They will also have expertise to pass on to you, should you choose to listen.

It's clear from the Sephiroth involved with these teacher guides that more intellectual pursuits will be overseen by the guides from Hod and more artistic ones by those from Netzach.

Either way, these teacher guides are there to help open up a true calling within, and they are very much of the moment, that's to say they are teachers for right now and will stay with you until you have learned all that you can, or perhaps all that you have chosen to remember. They will help with the great unravelling of your true calling.

Soul guides: Tiphareth

Next up the ladder are soul guides. These guides sometimes present themselves in costume to let you know what sort of energy they bring, and you won't have to struggle to decipher it, as they are reminding you of a higher vibration that's already set within you. They may not have a past-life link and they really aren't interested in personality issues of any sort. They look after many souls and usually move in when you're on a path to higher spiritual awareness, but not exclusively.

That leads me to answer that question: 'How do I contact my spirit guide?' If it's your soul guide you're after, and it usually is, you do it by raising your vibration through the work that you do. Then one day you'll get a glimpse of your guide, the next day a little bit more, and so on. They will respond to the effort you put into living from a sense of your higher spiritual principles.

Masters: Geburah and Chesed

I used to have a real problem with the hierarchy of guide this and Master that. It seemed that the spiritual worlds were run like some major company, with supervisors, managers, managing directors and of course the chief executive at the top of it all. And that corporate world was something I saw as Earthly and not something I enjoyed much on Earth either.

But without structure, there would be chaos; without defined roles, how would we know whom to turn to and why? And maybe, just maybe, the reason we have such structures here on Earth is another confirmation of 'as above, so below'.

Communicating with your guides

So, how do you ask your guides for help? Well, you ask your guides for help. It's not rocket science!

In fact, the secret to becoming more aware of your guides is communication. Even if you feel a bit silly asking for help from someone you can't see or hear, it's the start of getting the support you want.

By asking for help, you give permission for your guides to put ideas and thoughts into your head or to put people in front of you who will show you the way.

But this comes with a warning: if you ask for help and constantly ignore it, your guides will withdraw until it seems you're more likely to listen. You will be told three times and then they will step back, so it's up to you whether you action what you feel, no matter where it comes from, or not. Yes, that's *feel*. If you're expecting your guides to pop up through the floor and say, 'This way, please,' you may be sorely disappointed.

Or you may not. Some people do claim to see their guides physically every day. That hasn't been my experience, though. For most of us, they communicate through a feeling, a sensation that they are around. For me, that suggests that I stop and wait for any impressions to come to me. I do of course meditate specifically to meet my guides and to ask questions of them as well. I'll show you a very simple way of doing this, but first, which guide do you need?

The right guide for the right job

To recap, here are the guides and what they can help you with:

- *Earthly guides/Malkuth:* Friends and family, used for advice on Earthly matters.

- *Lifetime guide/Yesod:* A supportive guide with a link to the past and to the plan!

- *Doorkeeper/Yesod:* A protector who is always there defending your energy.

- *Teachers/Hod and Netzach:* For when you're learning new skills and remembering old skills. They move in and out.

- *Soul/Tiphareth:* For life's bigger questions. When you're ready, they are there.

- *Masters/Geburah and Chesed:* Highly evolved, these guides are waiting for you to pursue a spiritual path.

So much help is available and if you know what level your question is aimed at (and you do already), you will know which guide to ask.

Exercise: Asking your guides

How do you ask? Well, you can simply ask, as I mentioned earlier, either out loud or in your head, and know that you have been heard. If, however, you want to take the time to build stronger relationships with your guides then I would suggest you take some time out to meditate and raise yourself up to their level.

Here's a very simple visualization to help you establish contact. You have contact already? Even if you know who some of your guides are, maybe there are new ones waiting?

Switch off your phone and remove any distractions.

Light a candle, set your intention for doing the meditation and give thanks for the protection and guidance of the light.

- ❖ Relax, relax and close your eyes.

- ❖ Let all the tension go from your body. You can either clench each muscle, from the feet up, and let it go or you can just feel yourself sinking into the chair or the floor.

- ❖ Relax. Deep breathing can help – perhaps counting your breaths in rounds of 10...

❖ Now imagine you're in a forest. Build it around you and let it truly be there. You can touch the plants, smell the air and hear the noise of the forest around you...

❖ Ahead of you, you will see a path. Take it, it's a familiar and safe path for you to follow.

❖ An animal may dart out or fly around you. This is your animal guide, a guide that represents a facet of you. What is it? What does it mean?

❖ Walk along the path until you come to a clearing, a well-tended lawn with flowers planted around its border, all in the brightest colours you can imagine.

❖ In this clearing is a bench. It's a simple bench, but too inviting to ignore. Take a seat.

❖ Feel the peace of your surroundings, the calmness. Feel the sacredness of this moment.

❖ Within your meditation, imagine closing your eyes and asking your guide to give you a message, a feeling, an impression, perhaps an image of who they are.

❖ Take your time. Go with whatever you see, hear or feel.

❖ When you're ready, imagine opening your eyes and looking around the clearing, feeling happy at the contact you have made.

❖ When you feel the moment is right, prepare to leave. Before you do, say thank you to your guide. Always be respectful in these realms, always say thank you.

❖ Walk through the clearing and back along your path. Your animal guide may be there to show you back through the forest to where your journey began. Follow them.

❖ As you walk through the forest, say farewell and thank you to your animal and then carry on through the forest.

❖ Now let it fade away, let it fade, and bring your consciousness back into the here and now.

Write down your experience and remember, you will meet your guide again. If you didn't meet anyone, don't worry, they are there! Some people worry that if they don't see a guide, they don't have one. That's never, ever true.

If your guide gave you a gift, it may manifest here on Earth. Look out for it!

Chapter 5

Tarot and Planets

Return now to your drawing of the Tree. All those circles need to be linked by a network of paths. Each path has a specific meaning and as part of your journey they of course have a specific experience attached to them. Draw them in, just blank for now, and we will discuss their meanings in a moment.

When you've done that, look at the next drawing and notice the names on the paths. Do they remind you of anything?

Tarot

For those who study the Tarot, it will be very clear that these paths represent the 22 major arcana of the Tarot deck. Each path is named after one of those archetypes or symbols. As you would expect, they draw to you the experience of the card in question, just as meditating on the card would do, and knowing where you are and what you need next is why you would choose to walk that path. That will only be after you have built the Tree successfully on all your bodies, physical to metaphysical.

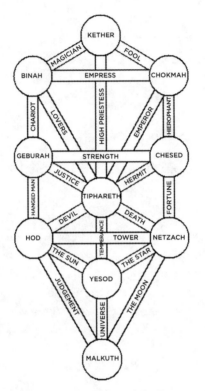

Figure 6: The Tree and the Tarot

The Sephiroth are sometimes referred to as paths too, but it's been my experience that the paths themselves are a different sort of energy. They can be pretty tough going!

If you read the Tarot, think about the names of the paths as you link the Sephiroth. If you don't, don't worry, the paths will become your teachers as the Tree of Life becomes your guide.

In some Tarot decks, the major arcana have different names. In my own Thoth deck the following paths are:

- Judgement: *Aeon*

- Temperance: *Art*

- Justice: *Adjustment*

- Strength: *Lust*

They hold the same qualities and share symbols, so don't be confused by this. Just go with what's on your own Tarot deck. If you don't have one, be guided to one and lose the thought that someone has to buy you one or it has to magically appear from thin air. Go get a deck, one you feel drawn to, and when you've got it, meditate with it around you and let the cards dance in your aura. Charge them with your energy.

As you can see, the paths run from each of the Sephiroth. They will be described in more detail later, but it's crucial to understand the basics of the Tree and to anchor it firmly *before* walking the paths, so let's concentrate on the Sephiroth for now.

The planets

Each of the Sephiroth is associated with a planet. This helps to understand its energy, but it also opens up the world of astrology to the student of Qabalah. A little astrological knowledge goes a long way.

Exercise: Planetary influences

Start with a print-out of a blank Tree of Life. If you can't copy it on your reader, remember there is one on the Qabalah drop down on my web page, davidwells.co.uk. If you can't download or print that, you can use the one you've already drawn.

If you already study astrology, still do this exercise. You will see each planet's influence in its Sephira and this will help you to store even more symbolism in the memory bank of your subconscious.

So let's begin.

Kether

❖ *Number:* One

❖ *Planet:* Neptune

❖ *Symbol:* ♆

Draw the symbol for Neptune on your Tree where Kether stands. It looks like a trident.

Neptune is the planet of mystery. It's veiled and sometimes hard to see behind. It governs magic and all things mystical; fitting, then, that it sits at the top of the Tree of Life. It's also a planet that can cause confusion and throw a veil over things so we have to work extra hard to see them.

Chokmah

❖ *Number:* Two

❖ *Planet:* Uranus

❖ *Symbol:* ♅

Now put this symbol where Chokmah sits. It's sort of like a television aerial, representing the electric force that comes from this planet, and is shown in this Sephira as it gives energy to your ideas, inspiring you and putting the spark of life onto the Tree. It takes no-thing and turns it into some-thing, and as a planet it can sometimes indicate where there may be disruption. But how often does disruption lead to new beginnings? Frequently.

Binah

- *Number:* Three
- *Planet:* Saturn
- *Symbol:* ♄

In Binah form is added. Saturn, with his rings around him, brings form to the Tree, and here in Binah the first rules are applied. It is by acknowledging the laws of the universe that all things come into manifestation. Get the rules in place, that's what Saturn asks, and where they aren't, things will be brought into order soon enough. Put his perfect form on your Tree. His. Notice this male planet represents the Great Mother. Binah is also polarity, the complementary aspect of opposites.

Chesed

- *Number:* Four
- *Planet:* Jupiter
- *Symbol:* ♃

The big four! Easy to remember, as it looks like a figure four. Jupiter is benevolent, he's the gift-giver and he offers abundance, but sometimes abundance is a hard one to deal with – abundance can lead to excess. This is where we can get carried away with the adventure. But Jupiter has a big smile, big pockets and a generous nature. Draw him on your Tree.

Geburah

- *Number:* Five
- *Planet:* Mars
- *Symbol:* ♂

Yes, it does look like the symbol for male. Fittingly, as Mars is the planet that governs war, anger, passion and sport. But he's also creative, active and wants us to get on with it! Here we look at what has to go, what confrontation has to happen so that things can run smoothly, what lessons have been learned and what lessons need to be delivered. Mars cuts away what's no longer required.

Tiphareth

* *Number:* Six
* *Planet:* The Sun
* *Symbol:* ☉

A circle with a dot in the centre, the Sun, our life's force and the balancing point on the Tree, the place where it can be reflected horizontally as well as vertically. This planet is one of healing, one that makes us all feel good when we feel its energy on us. It lights our way ahead. The Sun is also our will, where the strongest focus in our life is likely to be.

Netzach

* *Number:* Seven
* *Planet:* Venus
* *Symbol:* ♀

Yes, that's the symbol for female, funnily enough, and of course Venus is a female goddess. She is feminine energy, love and feelings, as well as all things nature. Often seen surrounded by animals, as well as wearing white, looking fabulous and generally being adored, she brings her grace and charm to Netzach. But make no mistake, she can (and does) bring tough love when required.

Hod

* *Number:* Eight
* *Planet:* Mercury
* *Symbol:* ☿

The talkative one, Mercury is the winged god of communication, the planet of images, and sits perfectly in Hod, where we create pictures before we manifest our dreams and goals. This boy is fleet of foot and can occasionally cause mischief, as we sometimes create images that aren't quite what we want, sometimes through fear and sometimes through advertising bombarding this planet to get us to buy stuff we don't really need! Be aware. And yes, when Mercury goes retrograde, or appears to go backwards in the heavens, everyone clutches their cardigans and gets ready for travel disruption.

Yesod

❖ *Number:* Nine

❖ *Planet:* The Moon

❖ *Symbol:* ☽

Please always draw as shown above – a happy Moon, one that is waxing, gaining power instead of losing it. The Moon is about our emotions, as distinct from our feelings. She is silvery, like a mirror, and holds more information in our subconscious than we will ever have time to use! Past-life work is often associated with Yesod and the Moon's influence is behind many of our reactions.

Malkuth

❖ *Number:* 10

❖ *Planet:* Earth

❖ *Symbol:* ⊗

This symbol represents the four elements. In our chart it's the Part of Fortune, where we will find most benefits in this life. It's a great indication of life purpose. Here, however, it really does remind us of the work we've just done. We're in a physical environment that gives form to all of the Sephiroth above it.

So now you have a Tree that has the planets on it, colour has entered the picture and all those images, together with the name, number and general influences of each Sephira, are starting to build a bigger picture.

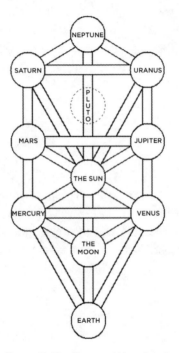

Figure 7: The Tree and the planets

Personal information

You are ruled by one of the Sephira. Consider your link:

- Kether is Pisces
- Chokmah is Aquarius

- Binah is Capricorn

- Chesed is Sagittarius

- Geburah is Aries and Scorpio

- Tiphareth is the Sun

- Netzach is Taurus and Libra

- Hod is Gemini and Virgo

- Yesod is Cancer

- Malkuth is your rising sign. Discoverable if you know your time of birth, this shows your approach to living here on Earth.

Think about what your personality Sephira offers you.

Exercise: Listening to your subconscious

Here is an opportunity to listen to what your subconscious is already telling you, based on the Tree of Life.

❖ Draw the Sephiroth again, but this time do it free-hand. Just draw 10 circles in order from one to 10. There's no need for the paths.

❖ Now look at the circles. Have you drawn one much bigger than the others? One much smaller? The small circle may denote which area needs more work, the larger where you may find it easier, but does that bring some complacency too?

Record your findings. Record your thoughts so far. Perhaps lay out some Tarot cards and have your natal (birth) chart printed.

Chapter 6

Understanding the Astrology

You don't need to be an astrologer, or want to be, to benefit from Qabalah, but there is much value to be gained from the planetary symbolism held within the Tree of Life and I'm sure you'll find those insights invaluable.

To help make it as easy as possible for you to use your natal chart, here are the symbols you'll find there and what they mean. You can find more information online. My own website has a chart calculator that explains what your own chart tells you, or you can use one of the many excellent websites out there, but if you can, visit an astrologer local to you. They will be able to help you too.

If you think this may all be a little complicated, please don't be put off. You'll only be looking at astrology when you consolidate the information from each Sephira (*see Part II*). In the next chapter I will go through a consolidation from beginning to end so you can see just how easy that can be.

Remember, finding out information from your chart is akin to pulling down part of the sacred contract you made before incarnation. Here are the symbols:

Astrological sign	Glyph
Aries	♈
Taurus	♉
Gemini	♊
Cancer	♋
Leo	♌
Virgo	♍
Libra	♎
Scorpio	♏
Sagittarius	♐
Capricorn	♑
Aquarius	♒
Pisces	♓

Planet	Glyph
Sun	☉
Moon	☽
Mercury	☿
Venus	♀
Mars	♂
Jupiter	♃
Saturn	♄
Uranus	♅
Neptune	♆
Pluto	♇
North Node	☊
South Node	☋

Planet	Glyph
Chiron	⚷
Ascendant	A^SC
MidHeaven	M^C
Part of Fortune	⊗
Earth	⊕

Aspect name	Glyph
Conjunction	☌
Opposition	☍
Trine	△
Square	□
Semi-Sextile	⌄
Sextile	⚹

These symbols, called glyphs, are easy to spot in your chart. What do they mean? Piecing it together is very simple: you take the planet, the sign and the house position it is in. The astrological wheel is divided into 12 houses, which correspond to different areas of life. Counting the first line on the left, the ascendant, as one, the first house, you can count along until you find the house, although to be honest they are usually numbered. For example:

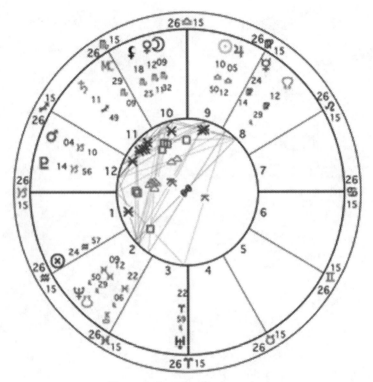

Figure 8: Sample astrology chart

Find the symbol for the Sun (a circle with a dot in the middle).

Which sign is it in? The symbol for the sign is underneath it. On this occasion it's Libra.

Which house is it in? Bit of a giveaway, as there's a great big number nine underneath it! Ninth house.

So the Sun is in Libra in the ninth house. You would use this information as part of your consolidation for Tiphareth, the Sephira of the Sun.

You can use your astrology book to find out what all the combinations of planets, signs and houses mean, or you can use the internet. Just remember to use a good site. There are some suggestions at the back of this book.

To find the meaning of the aspects in your chart (the angles, i.e. relationships, between the planets), I would use a good astrologer who can write them down for you or have a print-out of your chart done that includes them. This will take your astrological knowledge to another level and will be even more helpful, but for the purposes of your first look at the Tree of Life, the planet, the sign and the house position will more than suffice.

Chapter 7

Rituals in Life and on the Tree of Life

Ritual helps us transcend the physical and move into the realms of the meta-physical, that which is of a higher vibration.

Rituals are many and varied in magical practice. Some are simple and some extremely elaborate, but all have a purpose, an intention. Perhaps the most important thing is, what are you doing the ritual for?

'Because you've been told to' is never the answer. You may be shown a ritual or asked to take part in one, but unless you know what you're committing to, fully committing to, and why, please don't do it. Even if the person asking is yourself, your personality-self pushing buttons, you must ask *why* you want to do the ritual and what will it bring to you.

A ritual is a commitment, it's a definite statement put out into the astral worlds and beyond, and it will have your energy on it, so make no mistake, you are accountable for what you're doing. If you think it's just a bit of fun, you should definitely walk away. Ritual can be used for many things, but for a laugh is not one of them.

In this book you're going to do some meditations on the Sephiroth on a journey up the Tree of Life. You will get to know more about each Sephira in turn through visualizations and pathworkings and understand more about its energy and how it can influence your life.

Daily rituals

There are daily rituals I would recommend to help you on this journey:

- Take a Tarot or oracle card every day, learn about it and see how it predicts or affects your day. Record it in your journal.

- Before going to bed and when you get up in the morning, remind yourself of five things you're grateful for.

- Light a candle in the evening when you get in from work. See it as a way of cutting off from your working day and allowing yourself to rest.

- Take a salt bath at least once a week. Fill it with Epsom salts, relax and detox. It's as good for the soul as it is for the body.

- Every night before going to sleep, release any negative talk, self- or otherwise. Release it with love.

- Breathe. Sounds easy enough, but I mean consciously feel your breath moving in and out. Count it, deepen it and go to 100 breaths if you can. I use a 4-2-4-2 method of breathing, that's breathe in for the count of four, hold for two, out for four, hold for two and repeat.

- When you see or hear something that synchronizes with your study, make a note of it. Words are magical, remember that!

- On a full Moon, make a note of where the Moon is, in which astrological sign, and release something from your life you no longer need that's appropriate to the influence of the sign. This is another way of bringing astrology into your life. Make an extra effort when the Moon is in your Sun sign or Moon sign. Record how you feel on the full and new Moon.

- Perform the Qabalistic Cross ritual (*see below*) in the morning and at night for protection against energy loss and wandering into astral or Earthly areas you really shouldn't!

- The four great archangels also provide protection and energy and bring peace of mind to your meditations and pathworkings. We will look at those in a moment.

- A special mention for meditation: if you can meditate daily, that alone will transform you, and coupled with the growing energy of your Tree of Life journey? Wow!

The Qabalistic Cross

You will be working with the Qabalistic Cross to help protect your energy and empower your visualizations from here on in.

Exercise: The Qabalistic Cross

Begin the ritual facing East.

❖ Touch your forehead and vibrate (say with a load of oomph, a bit like when you hum): 'Ateh [A-Tay]'.

❖ Point towards your feet and vibrate 'Malkuth'.

❖ Touch your right shoulder and vibrate 'Ve-Geburah [Vay Ge-boo-ra]'.

❖ Touch your left shoulder and vibrate 'Ve-Gedulah [Vay Ge-doo-la]'.

❖ Place your hands together over your heart and vibrate 'Le-Olahm [Lay Oo-lam], Amen'.

This is simply 'As above, so below, the power and the glory, for ever and ever, amen', but it pre-dates Christianity by many thousands of years. It's the vibration of it that makes the difference, so really give it some oomph!

Working with ritual within the Sephiroth

Preparation tips

You need to prepare both yourself and the space you will be working in. Here are some tips:

• Check a Moon calendar and don't do any pathworkings three days prior to a new Moon. This phase is called the dark Moon and is not conducive to this sort of work.

• Eat about an hour or two beforehand, so you're not starving or bloated.

• Switch off all your phones.

- Find a comfortable spot to sit in. Don't lie down, as you might fall asleep!

- Let everyone know you can't be disturbed.

- Draw a Tarot card before you enter into the meditation.

- Light a candle with the intention of focusing on a particular Sephira or having a particular experience.

- Take a moment to breathe – nice and deep, in for a count of four, hold it for two, out for four seconds, hold it for two – a few times, each time relaxing more and more.

- Have no expectations. Approach each visualization like a child on an adventure.

To prepare yourself, try this very simple meditation to balance your chakras – your energy system. It's a great thing to do before working with any Sephira, as it helps you relax. In fact it's probably a good idea anytime!

Exercise: Chakra workout

This visualization is all about pushing energy around, helping it move, because movement is in itself a balancer. Think of it like riding a bike – the only way to keep moving forward is to maintain your balance.

Prepare to meditate.

- ❖ Close your eyes and visualize a white light around you. Make it as pure as you can.

- ❖ Now see a sphere of light above your head. Make it about the size of an apple and brilliant white.

- ✦ Next turn up the light even more. Make it blue white, sparkling and alive with energy. It's a representation of your higher self.

- ✦ Now imagine a lotus flower on your crown. Let the petals open up. Let them open wider.

- ✦ Next see a rosebud on your third eye, between your eyebrows in the centre of your forehead. Let it slowly open.

- ✦ Now see one on your throat and do the same.

- ✦ Now on your heart.

- ✦ When you've done that, let the light fall down through your legs and out through the soles of your feet.

- ✦ Let it move across your shoulders and out through the palms of your hands.

- ✦ Now the light is flowing in from your crown and out through your feet and palms. You're a being of light.

- ✦ Let that light balance you out, pushing away any grey bits. See them go and be replaced with balanced and vibrant energy.

- ✦ When you're ready, return the energy to your heart area. See it glow golden.

- ✦ See your beauty, feel your beauty, feel your balance.

- ✦ Let that golden light vibrate.

- ✦ Now push it up through your throat.

- ✦ Into your third eye.

- ✦ Through your crown.

- ✦ And back into the ball above your head.

- ✦ Now push that ball into the sky. Let it reconnect you to the universe.

❖ Now visualize all those rosebuds and the lotus flower returning to their natural resting place. They will feel recharged and clearer and will help you to feel the same.

Write down how you felt before and afterwards.

Setting up an altar

To make the most of your pathworkings, why not set up an altar? You can do this at any time – in fact I would encourage it! It will give you a focal point to work with and you can place items of relevance on it. For example, for Malkuth you might place fresh fruit, ivy leaves, flowers, symbols of the Earth and its beauty, and perhaps some herbs. In the chapters that follow, I have given suggestions for each Sephira, using what are called the correspondences.

When you're working on a Sephira, you might also like to set up your altar with its symbols, colours or whatever else comes to mind during the weeks or months you're working with its energy.

You can have seasonal altars too, for Midsummer, Samhain and Yule for example, full Moons, new Moons... The list is endless. Get creative, for in creativity your spirit thrives.

• Always have a central candle, which also acts as the candle for East, and a candle in each of the other quarters. That simply means one in the South, West and North to represent, respectively, Fire, Water and Earth. Your altar candle represents Air. More on those elements in a moment.

- To start a ritual, light them in a clockwise fashion, and when you have finished working, let them burn out safely. You don't have to leave them where they are, you can put them all on a tray. It's putting them out that's to be avoided if you can, but if you do have to put them out, do it in an anti-clockwise direction.

- Put an icon or symbol on your altar that speaks to you of the work you're doing, something like an Earth goddess or perhaps something that resonates with you in the description of each of the Sephiroth that follows.

- Burn incense that's relevant to the Sephira you're working on (*see the correspondences in the following chapters*).

Further preparation

What else do you need to do?

- When you do a pathworking, make an appointment, sit down and ask for the spiritual worlds to assist you at x o'clock and always, always be ready to start at that time. Ring a bell, as the sound of a bell can be heard in the astral worlds. Remember, it's a request for them to assist.

- Set up at least half an hour before to give time for the energy to build. Keep it going, once the candles are lit and the incense is burning, with music that's appropriate to the task in hand.

- Have a shower and put on clean, fresh clothing. If you can have something you wear only when pathworking then so much the better. Make it a plain colour at this point – white, or grey perhaps?

- Do the Qabalistic Cross (*see page 66*) then ask for the power of the four great archangels to stand in protection over you.

The archangels

These beings are real; respect must be given to them. Know what they look like, know what magical weapons they carry and see them carrying them:

- *Raphael* will be in yellow in front of you, carrying a sword, hilt up, or a fan for Air.

- *Michael* will be on your right, in reds, carrying a flaming wand for Fire.

- *Gabriel* will be behind you in blue, carrying a cup, a goblet, for Water.

- *Uriel* will be to your left, either in black or in the russet, brown and ochre colours of Earth, carrying a disk for Earth.

If it helps, see them in their respective colours as columns of light.

Exercise: Archangel protection ritual

❖ Taking a deep breath, raise and extend your arms up and out to your sides as if you were making a cross.

❖ Visualize four tall, robed and hooded figures surrounding you, each in a different direction.

❖   Say:

> *Before me RAPHAEL, behind me GABRIEL, to my*
> *right hand MICHAEL, to my left hand URIEL. Around*
> *me burn the pentagrams and behind me shines*
> *the six-rayed star of pure white brilliance.*

All of this will increase the energy to help you get a better experience and more clarity during your meditation. You'll see how it all fits together when you work with the Sephiroth in the following chapters.

There are other levels that you can take this to, but they are best left for another time. There's a very big difference between a visualization and a pathworking or Tree of Life meditation, and a very big difference between the ones in this book and more advanced pathworkings. You are at the beginning of your journey; don't run until you can walk, or you might stumble.

Releasing the energy

After your meditation, what then?

- When you have finished working, bow to the central altar and give thanks to each archangel in turn as you move anti-clockwise around the room, then make a final bow to the altar and leave.

- Collect yourself, maybe make some notes and then, when you are ready to break down the room completely, release the energy by walking around the room three times widdershins (anti-clockwise).

- See that energy move up into the universe to be used for positivity in the world.

Grounding your energy

It's essential to return to Earth properly and completely after any form of ritual, and in order to do that you must ground yourself. That simply means bringing your energy back and earthing it, but how?

- Make sure you eat and drink something.

- Do something mundane, like wash the dishes, do the ironing or go for a walk, and if it's appropriate, get your shoes off and walk on the Earth.

- Go for a swim or walk in the wind and rain.

- Gardening is a great way to ground yourself, and so too is having sex, but perhaps not whilst you're gardening!

- I know some people who've read some of my other books think it's funny when I say, 'Kettle on, biscuits out,' after each meditation, but it's such a useful practice. I won't be saying it after every meditation here, but you know I'll be thinking it.

- There are various crystals which will help with grounding too, but personally, I avoid anything magical and concentrate on anything with chocolate in it.

Part II

THE SEPHIROTH

Chapter 8

Malkuth

Before you begin getting to know this Sephira, please be mindful of the pace you take these sections at. I cannot stress enough that you must not only read each chapter, ponder the information, do any exercises and then, when you're ready, do the meditation for the Sephira, but you must also allow enough time for the energy of the Sephira to enter your life. Each one could take a month, maybe more, depending on how it comes into and affects your life, and if you rush things, you will trip yourself up.

With this in mind, let's start with Malkuth. It may seem odd to begin with the number 10, with what could be seen as the last Sephira on the Tree of Life, but this is where your consciousness resides in your physical body, right here, right now.

It's natural to assume that as this Sephira is the furthest away from the divine nature of Kether, it is somehow a diluted version of it, that the Sephiroth before have taken that divine energy and altered it so much that little of the original still exists. This is not true. The divine is in a blade of grass as well as in the greatest of archangels.

The Earth itself is a physical manifestation of the divine. When you put your feet on the ground, you can feel it beneath you; when you put food in your mouth, you can taste it. You know music is playing because you hear it, you know a painting is beautiful because you can see it, and when you pick a flower, you can smell its fragrance.

Next time you see someone leave litter or abuse Mother Earth in another way, consider that your anger isn't about their lack of respect for the Earth and her resources, but their lack of respect for the divine in you as well as in Gaia, the Earth.

But let's take it down a notch. Let's look at the way Malkuth shows itself in your life.

As Malkuth is the last of the Sephiroth, it contains the information and energy from all the nine that have gone before. Your personality, soul and spirit will have aligned to offer you the perfect experience here on Earth. So, health, cleanliness, exercise, money, perhaps security for you and your family, that feeling of wellbeing that comes from knowing you have it all sorted... Got that already?

Some people get it quicker than others; some feel they're never going to get everything running together and as one thing is sorted, another goes out of kilter, out of control. Perhaps that's true, but you can control your reaction, your attitude and what steps you take towards achieving your goals.

In *The Mystical Qabalah*, Dion Fortune says this of Malkuth:

> *If we try to escape from the discipline of matter, we are not advancing heaven-wards, but suffering from arrested development. – They find in cheap idealism an escape from the rigorous demands in life. But this is not a way of advancement, but a way of retreat.*

In other words – my words and I'm taking full responsibility for them:

> *It's wiser to face up to life on Earth, to grow spiritually through the planet you currently inhabit, than it is to constantly try to escape. We all know that running away from issues is impossible: they will either wait for you or follow you.*

You are here on Earth now. Every journey you make will start here, every one of them will end here, and you must be grounded, you must anchor your energy in Earth.

The Kingdom of Earth is a garden that needs tending and, as the gardener, it's down to you to make sure it's done. Help, advice, energy and even the plans are available to you from the Tree of Life, but only you can mow the lawn. You.

The elements

So, what is this garden made up of? We are all familiar with the four elements: Air, Fire, Water and Earth. They are easy to identify in their densest forms as the wind blowing through your hair, a fire warming you on a cold winter's day, water cleansing you or the Earth feeling firm beneath your bare feet. But in Malkuth these essential elements take on new meaning, new and magical life.

Here on Gaia, we see these mighty elements in all their beauty and in all their terror. Nature is mistress of the elements and nothing we can do can control her or these forces when they are unleashed. The same cannot be said for the esoteric representation of Air, Fire, Water and Earth. Here we do have control, although we don't always use it or admit to it.

Here's a little more about each of the elements:

Fire

Fire is an ancient symbol of power and divinity. Think of humanity's first discovery of fire and how incredible it must have been. But just how did it happen? Perhaps it was a lightning flash hitting a tree. How apt.

Ancient humans found the spark of fire in flint and in wood; they discovered how to release it and then how to use it. You too can get fired up by a project and want to release its full potential – and can you also get fired up when someone doesn't listen to a word you say? Both are uses of the Fire inherent within you rather than the obvious one external to you.

- Astrologically, the Fire signs are Aries, Leo and Sagittarius.
- In Tarot, Fire is represented by the suit of Wands.

Earth

Earth is what you stand on, the ground beneath your feet. The densest of the four elements, it is strong and supportive as well as dependable, and you can grow stuff in it!

When someone is described as being the 'earthy' sort, you know that means they are lovers of nature, guardians of trees, wear natural deodorant and knit their own blankets. Or is that a stereotype? Of course it is, but you get the point: you already know exactly how the element Earth shows itself in another human being, or at least some of them. Earthy individuals could also be practical, excel in financial matters, be great cooks and know their way around healthy living.

• Astrologically, the Earth signs are Taurus, Virgo and Capricorn.

• In Tarot, Earth is represented by the suit of Disks/ Pentacles.

Air

Air is the element that lifts you up on wings of supportive and encouraging words. It can also move around you unseen, like words spoken behind your back. Someone who is too airy for their own good will be no stranger to gossip.

Air is the full force of the storm as the howling winds confront you face on. It can be seen in the talkative sort who can use this mighty power to move mountains through big ideas and the ability to express them. Air can whisper or it can howl, but either way it's expressive, and proper use of the element of Air can change your mind or change your world.

- Astrologically, the Air signs are Gemini, Libra and Aquarius.

- In Tarot, Air is represented by the suit of Swords.

Water

Water always wins. It can harness the power of fire to create steam, it can cut through rock and earth, bring a seed to life and trap bubbles of air to lift it up, so it's no surprise that the element of Water represents love, emotions, your own subconscious, the tears of the universe and the weeping sorrow of loss. Guide it well, use it wisely and it will grow amazing things, quell storms and infuse your desires with a power so incredible nothing can resist them. Love always wins.

- Astrologically, the Water signs are Cancer, Scorpio and Pisces.

- In Tarot, Water is represented by the suit of Cups.

Balancing the elements

I have yet to meet anyone who is one element – every one of us is all four – but the strongest one is seen first, or makes itself known first perhaps? If someone is Airy, they may be seen as talkative; Fiery, they may have a temper; Watery, and it's the 'over-emotional' tag; and Earthy – practical and a bit dull perhaps?

Astrologically, the elements play a large part in the building of a natal chart. It's easy to count how many planets are in each element and often you'll hear people mention the lack of Earth, abundance of Air and so on in their chart.

Hopefully they are mentioning it as a gift, something to work with or work on, but sometimes they use it as an excuse: 'I can't help being angry, I have five planets in Fire!' That isn't an excuse. If you know it, then do something about it. Find a way to channel the creative, powerful and magnificent energy of Fire through work, sport or perhaps leadership.

Malkuth and the elements teach balance in all things, as does the Tree of Life. Finding what you need, what you desire to get a task done, isn't as easy as dialling up more Earth or turning down the heat, but noticing if you're overdoing one or the other will help you redress the balance, and that in turn will help you achieve your goals more quickly and with less resistance.

Ask yourself which element you think is dominant in your life. Are you Airy, Fiery, Watery or Earthy, and don't base it purely on your astrological sign, as we know there's much more to it than that!

I would reiterate that no matter what you find in your chart, it's how you direct the energy, how you adapt it and use it here on Earth, that makes the difference. And how you balance it out. This can be as simple as wearing the colour of an element you wish to attract – yellow for Air, red for Fire, blue for Water and brown for Earth.

Magical representation of the elements in Malkuth

In Malkuth you will meet the kings and the archangels associated with these forces. You will also meet the elementals, the magical representation of these beings here on Earth.

The elements are represented magically through the symbolic beings known as Sylphs (Air), Salamanders (Fire), Undines (Water) and Gnomes (Earth). In reality, the elements are pure energy – isn't everything? – but the elementals help call forward an element we require swiftly and clearly. The magical imagery of the elementals is an integral part of working with Qabalah.

Sylphs: Air

Air is represented by the Sylphs, fairy-like beings who direct the flow of Air. They move very quickly and are responsible for words, our mind and our ability to hear the elemental kingdoms and beyond. They purify the actual air we breathe, and with the metaphysical representation of Air, they purify our thoughts, or attempt to! If you felt heavy-headed, thick-headed, where would you go? For me, it would be to a beach on a windy day, as the Sylphs, the elementals of Air, bring clarity.

- The king of the Sylphs is Paralda, a cloud with piercing blue eyes of sapphire. He was one of the very first magical beings I saw with my own eyes, as he literally breathed air into me when I was extremely ill, and that illness signalled the beginning of my journey on the Tree of Life.

- The archangel of Air and the East is Raphael.

Salamanders: Fire

Fire is represented by the elemental beings called Salamanders. They appear as sparks of fire, burning bright with the power of creation. They're in the candle flame and the raging inferno. They work with their element not only physically, but also metaphysically in purifying us in the spiritual fires of lessons learned and power wielded.

These beings take a bright idea from the Sylphs and turn into action, take a plan and make it happen. Misuse of their energy on any level is a dangerous thing; at best it could be anger and at worst it could be catastrophic, as Fire destroys as well as creates. Be careful how you use all the elements, but this one in particular.

- The king of the Salamanders is Djinn. Volcanic with dark red and coal-like eyes, he has a commanding presence.

- As does the archangel of Fire and the South, Michael.

Undines: Water

Water is represented by the elemental beings called Undines. They are the sparkle on a wave, the magic of a babbling brook, the calm of an open body of water and the ferocity of waves crashing onto a beach on a stormy day.

Water is an emotional element. Sometimes it's seen in the gentleness of a moment of pure love, sometimes in tears when hearts break, or in the sobbing of loss or disappointment, and not just individually, but also in those moments when you grieve for humanity and the direction it's taking.

The Undines cleanse the oceans, just as they cleanse us through our emotional responses.

- The king of the Undines is Nixsa, a giant wave of energy the colour of the ocean.

- The archangel of Water and the West is Gabriel.

Gnomes: Earth

Earth is represented by the Gnomes. Forget the fishing rods and little red hats, for these hard-working elementals aren't anything like that! Here we meet the builders, those who bring the great plans of the mighty architect of the universe to fruition. They work tirelessly alongside their fellow elementals. The fact that we stand on solid ground, have earth that sustains life and largely have our waste products dealt with (in the face of overwhelming odds) is down to the Gnomes.

On a metaphysical level, they bring practical solutions in the areas of money, health and wellbeing. What could these be? Eat simply, eat well, buy from ethical sources, create little waste!

- The king of the Gnomes is Ghobe, a mighty Gnome who is not often seen, but whose presence can be felt.

- The archangel of Earth is Uriel of the North.

You will meet all these beings in your meditations. How they appear to you is how they appear to you; it's their energetic imprint that's important, rather than the images your mind puts around them. That's also important, yes, but how do they *feel* to you and have you felt that way before? You've always walked these paths, whether you've known it or not. The elementals have always been around you and you have felt their presence. This is all about remembering.

In a moment, some elemental homework for you, but in the meantime, for reference:

Element	Being	King	Archangel	Direction
Air	Sylph	Paralda	Raphael	East
Fire	Salamander	Djinn	Michael	South
Water	Undine	Nixsa	Gabriel	West
Earth	Gnome	Ghobe	Uriel	North

Exercise: Elemental homework

❖ Pause and consider your natural element. Do you think of yourself as airy? Earthy perhaps?

❖ If you have your natal chart, count the planets in Earth, Air, Fire and Water signs. Which one is truly dominant?

❖ What does that tell you about where you need to put more energy or look at how you spend it?

Angels

The archangel of Malkuth is Sandalphon. Legend tells us he's one of only two archangels who were once human. The other is his brother, Metatron. Sandalphon was the Old Testament prophet Elijah and Metatron was the patriarch Enoch.

Every journey you take up the Tree of Life begins and ends with Sandalphon. He touches you on the shoulder or the head as a symbol of his protection.

He is a mighty being, vast in size, so it's sometimes easier to feel his energy than attempt to 'see' him. Energy is, after all, what these great beings are made of. His image is often that of a young man wearing woollen robes, a symbol of simplicity and of earthliness. He wears sandals on his feet and they can often be heard on his approach.

It's tempting to imagine him stuck here on Earth, not able to move through the Tree, just waiting for us to turn up and pop into a Sephira or onto a path. Of course that's nothing like the truth of it! Sandalphon is the director of all the energies of the Tree, working with everyone from Metatron to the smallest spark of Salamander Fire energy to make the vision you are creating happen. Turn to him for help, for he knows you well. He knows your karmic conditions, your contract if you like, and he knows where help is needed and will support you even if he can't always deliver some of the changes you desire.

Why? Malkuth teaches us that whilst all this help is available, ultimately change is up to us as a collective and to each individual as part of that collective. Archangels and other helpers work *with*, not *for* us.

Vices and virtues

Each of the Sephiroth has a vice and a virtue associated with it, and the vice of Malkuth is inertia, which comes in many disguises. It's not all about closed curtains and chocolate-fuelled box-set marathons. Sometimes it comes in the brightest of guises. It can appear in the form of complacent idealism that thinks it's helping by sending love and light, without any further action or involvement.

This may be easier to see on a global level than a personal one, but this Tree of Life experience is your personal Tree, so where are you sending happy thoughts, hoping things will be okay and trusting that everything is as it should be when you know it's truly not and you need to break out of the prison of inertia and do something about it?

Don't confuse this process with keeping your vibrations positive, removing negative self-talk from your life or following a system that reminds you of your power. All are very valid. This is different. It's about telling yourself it will all work out and doing nothing to make that happen.

The virtue of Malkuth is discrimination – your ability to prioritize, to see what's needed first, what you can do right now and what will have to wait. This reminds you that you don't have to do everything at once. What is the most important thing today, right here, right now? Do it, no matter what. Any little change you make is a change and it's better than doing nothing at all.

Discrimination is also about understanding what's really happening. When the light burns so brightly it's all you can see, ask what's behind it, what's alongside it, and divert your gaze long enough to adjust to the truth – your truth.

Tarot cards

The four tens of the Tarot represent Malkuth energy and can be used to understand it better. They also represent the end. The deed is done, the task completed. If they constantly come up for you, perhaps Malkuth would be worth a visit? (*See below.*)

- *Ten of Wands:* Lord of Oppression. Sometimes an overbearing force focused on the gain of material things, but also the completion of the very same: a goal achieved.

- *Ten of Cups:* Lord of Satiety. Pleasure attained. Kindness, generosity and material happiness, but on occasion wastefulness.

- *Ten of Swords:* Lord of Ruin. Failure, disaster. Perhaps revelling in things going wrong. But also cleverness, quick-wittedness and persuasion.

- *Ten of Disks:* Lord of Wealth. Wealth, completion of a major project and yet maybe also a heaviness, a dullness when things are too practical.

When consolidating Malkuth (*page 99*), look for these cards. Their presence will add some significance to the experience of this Sephira for you.

Malkuth in life

Observe how you work on Earth. Where do you need to improve and how can you do that? The Tree of Life won't tell you what to do (nobody can do that and neither should they); what it will do is show you what needs to be learned, what improvements can be made and what great skills you bring to the Sephira you're working with.

In this case, take some time, observe your relationship with the planet you live on, the body you inhabit and the energies that make it so.

Visiting Malkuth

Every one of the Sephiroth has a temple or a way of working within it, a place of beauty, a place to go to begin magical journeys and a place in which to attract that particular energy into your life.

The nature of learning Qabalah without a teacher means that moving fully into temples may not be the easiest thing. So here the temple workings are kept simple. They will work at a level suitable to where you find yourself now. Each of you will have a unique way of experiencing them and bringing their energy to Earth. Remember there is no right or wrong thing to see when you visit the Sephiroth, and any prompts, symbols, feelings or insights are personal to you.

Correspondences

When, and only when, you feel ready to visit Malkuth, follow the advice on how to set everything up for the meditation (*page 69*). To help you dress your altar, here are some of the correspondences for Malkuth – things that represent it, colours, incense, etc. It's by no means the full list, but remember you don't have to have everything. It's about setting the scene, not being so attached to objects, bells and smells that you couldn't do it all in an empty room. If you can, do it!

- Keyword: Kingdom

- Number: 10

- Archangel: Sandalphon

- Order of angels: Ashim

- Planet: Earth

- Virtue: Discrimination

- Vice: Inertia, procrastination
- Gods/goddesses: Demeter, Freya, Lakshmi, Osiris, Persephone
- Colours: Brown, green, ochre, russet
- Crystals: Rock crystal, tiger's eye
- Incense: Dittany of Crete
- Body parts: The feet, the anus
- Tarot cards: The four tens, the princesses/pages

Exercise: The Malkuth temple

Dress your altar with lilies, ivy and willow.

Don't forget to take a Tarot card before your meditation.

When you're settled and have performed your opening protection ritual (Qabalistic Cross, archangels, *see pages 65–66 and 71–72*), you're ready to create the temple experience of Malkuth around you, and so too are the elementals, archangels and guides.

❖ Allow your usual surroundings to fade as you build a forest around you. Feel it, see it, smell it, touch it. Make it as real as you possibly can. Put your whole being into it.

❖ Walk along a path through the forest. If an animal comes your way, acknowledge it. This is a symbol, an aspect of yourself, or perhaps a power animal, a guide from the animal kingdom just for you. Find out what the animal represents symbolically and ask how that reflects in your life.

❖ Follow the path to a clearing, a well-kept place with flower borders and a beautiful lawn.

- At the far end you see a giant oak tree. It has an aura around it that sparkles in the light and it seems to vibrate in a magical way. Stop and feel that magic. It is magnificent. The Tree of Life.

- In its base is a great oak door with the symbol for Earth on it, a circle with a cross through it. It opens as you approach. Step inside.

- At first you notice the smell of damp earth and wood, then the smell of herbs fills your nostrils as you move into this space, the Temple of Malkuth.

- As you look down, you see herbs strewn across a black and white tiled floor. They release their fragrance as you walk over them.

- As your eyes become accustomed to the light, you see walls covered in oak and ahead of you a double-cubed altar with one cube of ebony and one of ivory.

- On the altar is a simple white cloth with a blue crystal bowl set upon it. In that bowl burns a flame.

- Ahead of the altar are two pillars, one of ebony on the left and one of ivory on the right, and behind them are three great doors of oak.

- On the eastern wall above those three great doors is a circular stained-glass window with the face of a man on it, symbolizing Aquarius and Air.

- To your right, in the South, there is another window with a lion rampant, symbolizing Leo and Fire.

- Behind you, in the West, is a window with a golden Sun with an eagle flying into it, symbolizing Scorpio and Water.

- And to your left, in the North, the window shows a black bull in a field of poppies, symbolizing Taurus and Earth.

- Stand in the centre of the temple and wait for Archangel Sandalphon.

- As he appears, the atmosphere changes. This humble and magnificent being comes towards you, his robe the colours of Earth – red, olive, brown – and seeming to weigh him down. The archangel of humanity is here, charged with your care.

- He smiles and welcomes you, asks you to face the eastern wall and places his hand on your shoulder or head in a blessing.

- As he steps back, he raises his hands and claps.

- From the eastern wall comes Paralda, a great billowing cloud of Air, and with him the Sylphs.

- From the southern wall comes Djinn, a wall of Fire with coal-black eyes, and with him the Salamanders.

- From the western wall comes a crashing wave of Water, Nixsa and his Undines.

- And from the northern wall comes Ghobe, his legions of Gnomes marching with order and purpose.

- All the elementals stand, waiting for their king's signal.

- The elemental kings step aside and you truly see how much Fire, Earth, Air and Water you currently have.

- What do you see? Are you busy with Water, empty of Fire? How are you made up right now?

- The elementals begin to move towards you. Don't be frightened. They dance around you, balancing you, helping you find to enthusiasm if Fire is lacking, to speak out if Air is in need of help, to be more practical and ordered if Earth is in need of cultivation, or perhaps to let go in a wave of Watery emotion.

- Soon they retreat, leaving you standing in the middle of the temple. Take a moment to reflect, to feel this peace and balance, to notice any ideas that are now flooding you as enthusiasm replaces apathy, solutions replace questions and you are now poised for action.

❖ Sandalphon appears, smiling. He embraces you and may offer you a gift, another symbol of your time here. If you do get one, remember to say thank you and find out what it means if the meaning isn't obvious at the time.

❖ He guides you out of the temple. It's okay, you can come back whenever you need to.

❖ As you leave the oak tree, the door closes behind you, and you, along with your animal if you've seen one, return to the clearing and then to the forest.

❖ Say farewell to your animal, let the forest fade and come back to the here and now.

Wiggle your fingers and your toes.

When you're ready, close down the energy, write up your notes, take a Tarot card and eat and drink something. No matter how small, it's symbolic of grounding your energy here on Earth.

How to consolidate each Sephira

When you reach the end of the lessons on each Sephira, you will consolidate your experience. Astrology will play a role here, and so too will the Tarot and your meditation. All form part of your personal experience of the Tree of Life.

When you sit down to do your consolidation, take another Tarot card. The consolidation will look like this:

Consolidation

Quote
To inspire you, a quote will be provided that's relevant to the Sephira in question.

'I have a dream...'
What are your intentions for the energy you are working so hard to draw to yourself? This is your dream. It will usually stay with you throughout your journey up the Tree. You can change it if you so desire, but take some time to get it right at the beginning if you can.

Astrology
A look at the relevant planet, its house and position, and what it tells you about the way the energy of the Sephira works for you.

Tarot cards
❖ *Going into the temple:* The card you chose before your meditation and what it means

❖ *Coming out of the temple:* The card you chose at the end of your meditation and what it means

❖ *Consolidating the temple card:* The card you chose when you sat down to do your consolidation and what it means

The route the cards are taking
What do the cards suggest to you? Put them all together. Find any common ground, any cards that are relevant to the Sephira you are consolidating, for example tens in Malkuth or fours in Chesed. Look at the suit, the number, the major arcana. Find any other relevant information. Then write a small paragraph on the cards, on the route they are taking.

Analysis of the temple visualization

Think about what you saw on your visit to the temple. What do the symbols mean to you? Which beings were more prominent? What did they say to you? How did you feel? All your emotional responses are important and highly relevant.

How it has manifested in your life

How has this shown itself in your life? (It *will* come into your life if it hasn't yet done so.) What has it made you think more about? What can you accept now that you couldn't before? What changes are you willing to make?

'Moving forward, I commit to...'

How will you use the lessons of this Sephira? How will you make sure you meet your goals? What will you do to make things happen?

Here's an example:

Malkuth consolidation

'The longest journey is the journey inwards. Of him who has chosen his destiny, who has started upon his quest for the source of his being.'

DAG HAMMARSKJÖLD

'I have a dream...'

...of becoming self-employed, of living my life in accordance with my own goals, dreams and spiritual ideals.

Astrology

The Part of Fortune (not a planet but it represents Earth in your chart). In the sample astrology chart (*see page 60*) it's in Aquarius, in the first house. So I will benefit from having my independence and through showing up in the world as the unique individual that I am.

Tarot cards

❖ *Going into the temple:* Princess/Page of Cups. Dreams can come true, listen to your intuition.

❖ *Coming out of the temple:* Three of Cups. Seeds are sown for a bright harvest.

❖ *Consolidating the temple:* Ace of Swords. A new way of thinking, clear ideas.

The route the cards are taking

If I listen to my intuition, my dreams can come true. I can go sow those seeds, those ideas, and watch them flourish!

Analysis of the temple visualization

I saw the Archangel Sandalphon. He handed me an acorn, a golden acorn, and when the elemental beings visited, I saw mainly Earth. I took this to mean there is hard work ahead, but from tiny acorns mighty oaks grow!

How it has manifested in your life

Work has been hard going and I have been thinking about what it would be like to be my own boss. I know it takes time and I am being patient, but I am also making plans so that when the time is right I will be ready. I am not being inert, doing nothing about it all. Already I have heard of a premises that may be available in 10 months' time and I am thinking about how I could be in a position to buy it and working towards that. I also feel fitter and healthier and have become more in charge of my energy by looking at what I eat and how I exercise.

'Moving forward, I commit to...'
Paying more attention to my physical needs and not allowing myself to fall into the trap of inertia.

Now it's your turn!

Malkuth consolidation

'The longest journey is the journey inwards. Of him who has chosen his destiny, who has started upon his quest for the source of his being.'
DAG HAMMARSKJÖLD

'I have a dream...'
What is your dream? What do you want from your journey?

Astrology
Where is the Part of Fortune in your chart (denoted by a circle with a cross in the centre of it)? What does that tell you?

Tarot cards
❖ Going into the temple: Card

❖ Coming out of the temple: Card

❖ Consolidating the temple: Card

The route the cards are taking
A short analysis of what the cards tell you.

Analysis of the temple visualization
How you felt, what you saw, what the symbols mean to you.

How it has manifested in your life
How has it presented itself in your life here on Earth? What have you noticed that you missed before? What do you want to change?

'Moving forward, I commit to...'
Make a commitment to making those changes happen.

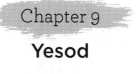

Chapter 9

Yesod

In recent years there has been a great resurgence of interest in mediumship, the paranormal and all things ghostly. Things that go bump in the night are separated from our Earthly world by a thin veil, just as Malkuth is separated from Yesod, and the physical world of Assiah is separated from Yetzirah, the world of angels and astral travellers. The next plane of existence, sometimes called the astral plane, is the domain of Yesod and we cannot travel up or down the Tree to and from Malkuth without moving past these worlds.

In their simplest forms, they are where you find deceased relations waiting for you, their memories still within you and signs coming from them, from Yesod to Malkuth, from the astral worlds to that smile on your face as you think of them here on Earth. All well and good, but the Tree of Life has other things in mind.

Yesod is where you meet your powerful subconscious mind, where you reach into that melting pot of all you've ever done to bring forth some answers that will help you in the here and now, as well as some lessons you might still have to work on.

I'm all for living in the now, being positive and keeping things going to maintain impetus as you move towards your goals, but the reality is that along the way you'll have things you want to confront. Some folks glibly say, 'Forget it, it's not important, move on,' but all that does is push what has made itself known under the astral carpet until eventually you're not able to move on without tripping over it.

So this is where you give birth to all those thoughts, feelings and emotions and where you remind yourself of what's waiting for you and also what to be wary of as you prepare for that birth. It's where you examine the cycles and habits that you might want to work on before you go any further.

Yesod's association with the Moon reminds us that life itself moves in cycles. There is a time to move forward, a time to lie low, a time to talk, a time to remain silent, a time to remember and a time to forget and truly move on. Yesod is called the Foundation because it turns the wheels of the universe to bring us what we want in the way we've seen it, felt it and indeed worked for it.

Mirrors are Yesod, elephants are Yesod, and so is the herb rosemary, which is said to be for remembrance, if you remember your Shakespeare. The mirror reflects back, but it's also seen in many meditations as a portal to your own subconscious. Indeed, I use it in just that way in past-life workshops. And the elephant? It never forgets. Neither does your subconscious. So, when you're dressing your Yesod altar, think about using a mirror, a statue of an elephant (a real one would probably break it) and some rosemary, much loved of Ophelia in *Hamlet*. Recent studies at Northumberland University in the UK saw significant memory gains in people who were placed in a room infused with its fragrance. That's also a reminder that much of what's on the Tree of Life is already in place in your life; there will be more.

The path that links Yesod to Malkuth is called the Universe path. The Universe is one of the major arcana of the Tarot, of course. In fact it's the last card, the end of the journey, the birth canal, the manifestation of your hard work – and work is what Yesod recognizes, the effort you've put in and how much you understand the workings of the vision of the machinery of the universe. It's easy to think of that as cogs and wheels, or maybe not. Perhaps you think of it as angels, spirit guides and relations who have passed over, or as thoughts, feelings and emotions. They're all right.

The lightning flash

Yesod is reactive, it works through the lightning flash by gathering all the information you are directing into the physical world through your imagination and your ability to see it, believe it, conceive it. Using symbols, clear words and directed action, you are giving life to what you want to create.

So you're seeing the land of dreams and what can be, but it must be activated by the magic, and that resides in the words, the spell-ing, of Hod, above. Yesod's job is to bring it to birth – a very important point. What are you creating with your thoughts and emotions?

As the magic awakens in you, it's very exciting. You can have whatever you want, you just have to think it, do a bit of woo-woo and there it is. Not quite. Here's where you come up against what you want versus what you need, and what about what the universe needs? Maybe the universe needs you to wait a while?

Once you understand that, true peace comes. The waters of Yesod are still there for you to catch more than your fair share of come-true-fish but, as the rest of your journey will show you, what you think will solve all your problems now may not be the true will of your soul. Find that first.

Angels

Gabriel is the angel of Yesod. He is the archangel of Water, and Yesod is associated with Cancer and emotional energy. He is also the archangel we see at the annunciation, when Mary is told of the coming birth. Here he sits in governance over the birth canal on the Tree of Life, ready to manifest your dreams.

The order of angels you meet here are the Cherubim. They help lay the foundations of the material universe you see around you. They keep the plans and hold the patterns. They are the architects, whilst the elementals of Malkuth are the builders.

Vices and virtues

Idleness is the vice, as contentment can sometimes lead to sitting back and changing nothing. Then your wheels clog up, but life is about keeping things moving and being open to change.

From that comes independence, the virtue of Yesod, where you are master of your own machine. Independence means freedom from the restrictions of the physical world as you allow yourself to fly in these realms. The building of a house takes years in the physical world, but here it takes a second. But don't get overly keen – to manifest what you see here you must know the secrets of the Sephira above. It will ever be so.

Tarot cards

The four nines remind you that you are almost there, the hard work is done and you're just about to reap the benefits, but as ever there are warnings: don't give in to unnecessary worry and keep the images of what you want sharp, well defined and clear.

- *Nine of Wands:* Lord of Strength. Power, a steady force, success after strife and hard work. You've got what it takes.

- *Nine of Swords:* Lord of Cruelty. Sometimes the negativity of others, but sometimes your own negative self-talk. Do you do that?

- *Nine of Cups:* Lord of Happiness. No matter what's going on in your life, there is beauty around you. Happiness is a choice.

- *Nine of Disks:* Lord of Gain. A chance to end a job, to find solutions and to serve for no other reason than service itself.

Yesod in life

In life, Yesod is likely to show itself through cycles, those repeat performances that we all go through, and taking some time to think about those is what's asked of you now. Which cycles or habits work really well for you and which would you like to break free from?

What Yesod is not about is regret. You may recognize where you could have done things differently, but all experiences are valid and workable, and when you do work with them, the wheels turn again and the great mechanism of the universe brings forth new and exciting things.

Remember, Qabalah can be learned, and it can be repeated with great knowledge, with every fine detail well understood, but no matter how great or small your knowledge, it's going nowhere unless you make it practical, unless you bring it into this physical world.

Exercise: A Moon diary

Get yourself a Moon diary and look at the phases of the Moon. When is she waxing? When is she waning, full and new? And how you feel when she's in each of those cycles? Chart your emotions using the diary and see if the Moon offers up any insight into your behaviour. Reflect on those habits and cycles.

Three days before a new Moon is called a dark Moon. Please do nothing on those days – well, nothing magical that is, unless it's finding time to reflect on what you'd like from the new Moon, depending on where she is and where that affects you in your own chart, or simply how it makes you feel. Think about what you want to give birth to here on Earth and what you'd rather not repeat.

The pull of the Moon and the vision of a full Moon will never be the same again as you understand her magic more.

Visiting Yesod

Correspondences

Let's start with some correspondences:

- *Keyword:* Foundation

- *Number:* Nine

- *Archangel:* Gabriel

- *Order of angels:* Cherubim

- *Planet:* The Moon

- *Virtue:* Independence

- *Vice:* Idleness

- *Gods/goddesses:* Artemis, Diana, Ganesha, Isis, Mani

- *Colour:* Violet

- *Crystals:* Moonstone, pearl, quartz

- *Incense:* Jasmine

- *Body part:* Genitals

- *Tarot cards:* The four nines

Exercise: The Temple of Yesod

Decorate your altar, set up your room as usual, burn jasmine incense, take a Tarot card and remember to allow yourself some time to be still and to let the energy of the room build.

As you are taking one step further up the Tree, it's worth pausing to remember that as you do so, you're not only moving into Yesod's realms, you're also beginning to feel those of Hod and Netzach more closely. But for now, the route to your Yesod experience awaits.

Whilst these aren't full temple workings, they are still effective, as even just reading the text of the Sephira has no doubt been. So, don't enter the temple without having thought about the effects of Yesod and the forces it contains.

Perform your cleansing and protection ritual. Remember that Gabriel is the archangel of this Sephira.

Do any opening up of your energy you wish to do, working with the chakras or moving energy around your body (see page 67).

Ask for the assistance of Gabriel and your guides. Become aware of them around you.

Breathe in the 4-2-4-2 rhythm to take yourself into a full meditative state of being.

❖ Allow your normal surroundings to fade. The material world gives way as you enter the astral worlds...

❖ See yourself in the magical forest of Malkuth. Smell it, hear it, touch it and be a part of it.

❖ Follow the path to the Tree of Life itself. There it is, vibrating and shining, singing its song as you approach.

❖ In the clearing, pause a moment. You'll see a moonstone move away from the branches of the Tree, and as it moves closer to you, it forms a sphere of purple and silver light and draws you towards it.

❖ As you move towards it, offer the symbol for the Moon, the crescent shape, the great luminary, and when you're ready, enter the sphere of light.

❖ Within this world you can see the astral template of every being, of every plant, of every thing – a glowing light.

❖ You hear the running water of a brook, and the sounds of the oceans, and as you move through this world, begin to become aware of movement ahead of you.

❖ Walk on until you see the Temple of Yesod in the distance. How does your temple appear? Is it a silver pagoda, splendid in the moonlight? Perhaps it's a simpler building of white, silver and purple light?

❖ Nine sides form the shape of the building and in its garden of magical light the beings of Yesod gather to commune with you.

❖ Who is there? The goddess of the Moon, or Gabriel himself perhaps? Ask for information that's appropriate to you right here, right now, and will be safe and understandable when you take it back into the realms of Malkuth.

❖ Perhaps you catch a glimpse of the workings of the machinery of the universe?

❖ You may see people from your past lives, or some from this life who have crossed from the mortal realms.

❖ When you have finished communing with your hosts, they may offer you a gift, a reminder of your visit to these realms. Return their kindness with a promise made to work with and respect the power of this Sephira in your own life and on your own Tree.

❖ Now it's time to leave. Walk back down the path, giving thanks for the experience and paying respect to your guides.

❖ You find yourself back in the clearing as the doorway to the experience of Yesod returns to the Tree.

❖ As you walk through the temple forest, begin to bring your awareness back into the room. Return to your usual surroundings.

When you have closed your meditation down, take a Tarot card, make notes and remember to eat and drink something. No matter how small, it's symbolic of grounding your energy here on Earth.

Your consolidation sheet follows.

Yesod consolidation

'The subconscious is ceaselessly murmuring, and it is by listening to these murmurs that one hears the truth.'

GASTON BACHELARD, FRENCH PHILOSOPHER

'I have a dream...'
Remind yourself of the dream you stated in Malkuth.

Astrology
The Moon. How does your subconscious work? What lies behind your actions here on Earth?

Find the Moon in your natal chart. What sign is she in and what planets affect her?

Tarot cards
❖ Going into the temple: Card

- ❖ Coming out of the temple: Card

- ❖ Consolidating the temple: Card

The route the cards are taking
A short analysis of what the cards tell you.

Analysis of the temple visualization
How you felt, what you saw, what the symbols mean to you.

How it has manifested in your life
How has it presented itself in your life here on Earth? What have you noticed that you missed before? What do you want to change?

'Moving forward, I commit to...'
Make a commitment to making those changes happen.

Chapter 10

Hod

Here you meet the first of the Sephira at the base of the Pillar of Severity, the first Sephira to face the Pillar of Mercy, through its direct opposite, Netzach. You are now in the world of thoughts, the world of consciousness, language and the mind.

Explaining how the mind works is impossible. Who knows it all? But perhaps that's how it should be? As you delve into the world of Hod, you'll have more questions than answers about the eternal mystery of the human condition and the journey you're currently on.

Just as the Tree of Life vibrates and changes with each Sephira you visit but remains constant, so do you. Remember you are a tree, amongst the many trees that make up the universe, and you too vibrate, you have a song. Sometimes that song isn't as clear or as beautiful as you'd like, I guess, but you also have a base note, a constant sound that identifies you. This announces your presence in the universe and helps to make up the sound of Earth, of Malkuth, and the overall song of the universe.

You know you can change the tone. You can raise it when you feel it's been lowered, and there are many ways to do that, but the one thing that has stuck with me from the moment I first heard it is this: 'The one thing you can always change is your attitude.' Your tone, your song, your whole vibration shifts when you approach things differently.

In Hod you will bring about changes in your life by changing your attitude, shifting the way you think, conquering negative self-talk and inviting in the new. This is the realm of active magic, of conjuring new things into your life via techniques that draw down the Tree above you and offer it up to the world of Yesod to be brought into manifestation in Malkuth. What you think, you become.

Your mind can create images so powerful that your physical body will react as if what you've thought has actually happened. Imagine eating a lemon and your mouth will water. There are authors who have explored the mind–body link in great detail and it may be worth your time seeking out what they have written.

Ceremony and planning also live in Hod – how you go about making things happen, all the details, as well as who stands where and when. This is the organizational Sephira, but such is the nature of Hod, and of Mercury, its planetary force, that it's also very fluid and can sometimes go off on a tangent. Who hasn't had a great idea, only to sideline it in favour of something sparkling in the distance? If you find yourself sidelined, meditating on Hod can put you back on track.

The next Sephira, Netzach, is all about feelings, while Hod is form. If you look at your Tarot tree, you'll see that the path between them is The Tower card. If you veer towards over-thinking things, or over-feeling them, you easily bring about the collapse of that tower and you have to start to build all over again. I'm sure, like most of us, you find that happening often. Balancing thoughts and feelings is one of the things that we humans are always attempting to do! So, how do you do it? How do you stop living in your mind at the expense of everything else?

Whose mind is it anyway?

Much of what you see around you came into manifestation through someone's mind. Those buildings were planned on a drawing board, that meal was put together by someone thinking up great ways with kale (thanks for that). The clothes you wear, the sofa you sit on, and so it goes on... But what about the way *you* look at the world, the way *you* perceive it? Are those your thoughts or are they someone else's? Do you think the news you listen to at breakfast time is magically plucked from thin air or does a human being decide what you hear and how you hear it?

What can you do about that? You know: change your attitude. Change the way you filter information and the way you react to it, or perhaps get rid of it altogether by meditating on your awesomeness before going to work rather than listening to the thoughts, fears and choices of a news editor. Make no mistake, it's a human being making that choice for you, it's not an organization, a faceless thing, it's someone with an opinion, someone with a name and a face.

Whilst I would agree that your thoughts create your world, there are plenty of other people's thoughts interfering with that process if you allow them. So maybe the gift of Hod isn't just the ability to create through language, thought and the beauty of your words, but also the ability to see who is pushing their agenda onto you.

Sharing your vision

In any kind of ritual work, you give form and life to the images that you work with. For example, when working with angelic forces, you give them a shape, a colour, a name and even a personality, all through the process of Hod. You therefore do exactly same thing with negative processes and you should be wary of those who seek to impose those negative images on you.

However, no Sephira can work on its own and in order to make these images truly come alive, the forces in all the Sephiroth above and below come into play. If we look at those immediately surrounding Hod, we see that opposite is Netzach, which is predominantly about feelings, as you will see in the next chapter, while directly below Hod is Yesod, which is about emotions. This is a great example of how the Sephiroth work together. Feelings can be given shape through Hod and given life through the emotional desire to see them manifest. You create your own images and you always will, and your mind works best with symbols and images. Some would say it works no other way.

With that in mind, it's perhaps a good idea to find out what images, symbols and pictures you have in your head! What do you want from your journey on the Tree? Remember that even though you were asked to state your dream in your earlier consolidations, you can change it should you wish. Perhaps the following exercise may help you clarify what it is you truly want – that's 'want' as opposed to 'need'.

Exercise: Vision bored

I know, 'vision *board*' – or maybe you feel it is more 'bored'? However, bear with, it's going to be slightly different this time. This is an exercise to help you see where you are now, what needs to be done to shift any negative self-talk and what direct action can be taken. So maybe it's better described as your 'Hod board'.

Look at the categories below. By collecting images that describe them, you can put together an honest appraisal of where you are and what has to happen. And therefore where a change in attitude is to be encouraged.

Take into account that not everything will go to plan – your plan, that is. There is a universal one, and another 70 billion humans who could all put together a vision board if they had the peace, food, water, opportunity, time, support and love to do so.

But this is about where you are now. So, scour the internet for images, cut up your magazines or draw lovely things from your wonderful imagination, and use colour, lots of colour, and don't be afraid to go grey as well, to go dark on what doesn't lighten your load. Call it what it is.

❖ Who or what are you responsible for – your kids, the mortgage, pets, etc. What images represent how you feel about that? Be honest. If it feels too much sometimes, ask why you're not getting help. Have you asked?

❖ Where's your moral compass at? What really gets on your nerves about the way people treat each other? On the other hand, what do you love to see? What restores your faith in humanity and reminds you that there are indeed some wonderful people on this planet?

- ❖ What now? See the game – put up images that expose those who play with your thoughts, who tell you what to think and what nonsense to spend your hard-earned cash on. Put up images of what you no longer need in your life because selling it to you was someone else's plan.

- ❖ Your past now – what you've achieved, what you've overcome and how great you felt when it was all over. Hard times come to us all; how you approach them is often a real test for Hod and the realms of the mind.

- ❖ What you want to achieve is next – what's the new plan for you and yours? Make it as grand as you want – it's you who's going to make it happen. Here you can let your imagination go wild. Give it free rein and put every happy thought and sparkle of mind glitter into those images.

- ❖ See the work you need to do to make it happen, but most importantly, see the next step. What images conjure up the next step for you? Be realistic – a grand goal won't change, but the way you dance towards it might have to.

Now you have a board, it will remind you not only of your goals but also of what you've done to be where you are now, what responsibilities you have and whether you need to share them, what's next and what has to happen to get things started.

Change the board when you feel the need. Tear things off with glee when you've achieved them or you're finally ready to let them go, and stick new and wonderful things on it when you're ready to attract more of them. Never let it be boring.

Angels

The archangel of Hod is sometimes said to be Raphael, sometimes Michael, and both are referenced in the Sephira of Tiphareth too, so perhaps they are interchangeable? Perhaps not. Sometimes you'll see both. Raphael is the archangel of Air, and suits this temple's focus on the mind, but Michael fights for truth, and here you must produce truthful images – your real desires – lest you manifest someone else's. So you must use whichever archangel you think is best suited to your situation. In the visualization that follows, it is Michael.

The heavenly host are the Ben Elohim, children of God/dess.

Vices and virtues

The vice of Hod is falsehood and dishonesty. Images can be created to confuse and to distract – and they are, frequently.

Its virtue is truthfulness. Even when it's not easy to speak the truth or to admit to it in the realms of our own mind, we all know that being truthful sets us free. Ponder on that a moment.

Tarot cards

If you're a Tarot reader, you'll know that in the major arcana the symbol for infinity, the number eight on its side, sits above The Magician's head. Eight is the number for Hod. The clues are and have always been there, hidden in plain sight, and as you begin to realize this, you'll no doubt begin to notice more.

So, the four eights represent Hod and they are:

- *Eight of Wands:* The Lord of Swiftness. A direct image of clarity and what should happen next. A vision of a new phase in your life.

- *Eight of Cups:* The Lord of Indolence. Look for those who impose their will more than you do your own. They may take your energy, or rather you may give it away.

- *Eight of Swords:* The Lord of Interference. Things may not be going your way. Perhaps step away and do something else?

- *Eight of Disks:* The Lord of Prudence. Be ready for an opportunity, but also ready to work with any stress or change required.

Visiting Hod

In this temple you'll be asked to make a commitment – a commitment to the path ahead. That can mean many things. For me, it meant committing to working with the Tree of Life, to my own spiritual unfolding and to teaching in whichever way I could.

Before visiting this temple then, consider what you're going to contribute to the Tree of Life and how you're going to use your new knowledge in the here and now. You'll be asked to make that commitment, to visualize yourself writing it and then burning it. Whenever I see myself doing this in visualizations, I always follow it through by doing the same here on Earth. Find a safe place to burn your paper and watch the sparks, the Salamanders, take it heavenwards!

Correspondences

- *Keyword:* Splendour

- *Number:* Eight

- *Archangel:* Michael or Raphael

- *Order of angels:* Ben Elohim

- *Planet:* Mercury

- *Virtue:* Truthfulness

- *Vice:* Dishonesty, falsehood

- *Gods/goddesses:* Hanuman, Mercury, Merlin, Thoth

- *Colour:* Orange

- *Crystals:* Agate, opal

- *Incense:* Storax, white sandalwood

- *Body part:* Legs, loins

- *Tarot cards:* The four eights

Exercise: The Temple of Hod

Remember to perform your opening ritual and dress your altar accordingly, and on this occasion to have your commitment ready. You can either remember it or have it written down and glance at it during the visualization. Either way, it's a good idea to have it in written form on your altar. Remember, you're not physically burning it during this visualization. If you want to do that, do it afterwards, and take it seriously. You'll be held to account as you send your words skywards.

Don't forget to take a Tarot card before your meditation.

Perform your usual protection and opening procedure.

Ask your guides for their support. The archangel of Hod is Michael or Raphael.

Breathe in the 4-2-4-2 rhythm and ask for the forces of Hod to meet you in whichever way is appropriate to you right here, right now.

❖ Let the material world disappear around you and begin to build the magical temple garden that is already so familiar to you.

❖ Use all your senses – feel the grass beneath your feet, the wind on your skin and the warmth of the Sun on your body. Smell the wonderful fragrances of the forest.

❖ See your Tree of Life. Watch it sway and sing your soul's song in the wind as it calls you to it.

❖ The crystals in its branches shift to an orange colour and an orange agate breaks from the Tree to form a sphere, a gateway to the temple garden of Hod.

❖ As you approach the sphere of orange light, you see it is shot with quicksilver. Its beauty reminds you of butterflies' wings.

❖ Enter the sphere. Use the symbol for Mercury or perhaps the name of the archangel.

❖ As you walk into the sphere, your mind wakes up, your vision clears and your thoughts are sharper than they have ever been. You're wide awake, fully awake, open to the truths that will present themselves to you as you walk in the garden of Hod.

❖ You meet the symbols and creatures of Hod. Some will have a message for you and they will deliver it quickly and accurately.

❖ As you walk further, carry on communing with any beings you meet. Feel their words, see their vibrations and colours.

❖ Words may dance in front of you – words you have used. Which ones are dull, which ones hold little light, which ones are no longer needed?

❖ See the bright words, dance with the brightest of the bright words and let them move through you. Hold them close, remember them.

❖ You see the Temple of Hod ahead of you. What does your Hod look like? Sometimes it's an ice palace, sometimes it's a giant library or great hall of learning. Whatever it is, it's your Hod.

❖ From the temple, Archangel Michael comes towards you.

❖ Commune with him. Listen to what he has to tell you. Ask for information on Hod and how it works, its virtue perhaps. Ask for clarity. Perhaps you need help with your commitment?

❖ As you walk with the archangels and the hosts and beings of Hod, they will guide you to a brazier, a fire burning brightly.

❖ A Sylph-like creature will hand you a blank piece of parchment for you to write down your commitment.

❖ You have no pen? Imagine, imagine and the words will appear on the page as your imagination manifests your thoughts through the worlds of Yesod.

❖ When your words have appeared, burn the parchment in the brazier and watch your words be released and float up the Tree of Life.

❖ When you have finished communing with your hosts, they may offer you a gift, a reminder of your visit to these realms. Return their kindness with a promise to work with and respect the power of this Sephira in your own life and on your own Tree.

❖ Perhaps you catch a glimpse of a vision of splendour and how that looks to you on your path right now, how it shows itself in your life.

❖ Say your farewells and follow the path back to your orange sphere and into the garden of Malkuth, considering what you have learned, what you want to action when you return and how language affects your very being, your human being.

❖ See, feel, hear and smell the temple forest around you, and when you're ready, let it fade and bring your consciousness back to the here and now.

Close your meditation with the same respect you opened it with and record your journey. Remember to eat and drink and take a Tarot card.

―――――――――――――――――――――――――――――――――――

Using your notes and the symbolism of the path, complete your consolidation of Hod:

Hod consolidation

'As a single footstep will not make a path on the Earth, so a single thought will not make a pathway in the mind. To make a deep physical path, we walk again and again. To make a deep mental path, we must think over and over the kind of thoughts we wish to dominate our lives.'
HENRY DAVID THOREAU

'I have a dream…'
Remind yourself of the dream you stated in Malkuth.

Astrology
Look at Mercury in your chart. Which sign is it in? What does it tell you about the way your mind works?

Tarot cards
❖ Going into the temple: Card

❖ Coming out of the temple: Card

❖ Consolidating the temple: Card

The route the cards are taking
A short analysis of what the cards tell you.

Analysis of the temple visualization
How you felt, what you saw, what the symbols mean to you.

How it has manifested in your life
How has it presented itself in your life here on Earth? What have you noticed that you missed before? What do you want to change?

'Moving forward, I commit to...'
Make a commitment to making those changes happen.

Chapter 11

Netzach

Welcome to the realms of nature, of feelings, Venus and of course love! But before you embark upon this part of your journey, this is perhaps a good place to pause and consider where Netzach sits on the Tree of Life. If you look at your drawings so far, you will see Netzach sits opposite Hod and at the base of the Pillar of Mercy. It represents instincts, feelings and, as you have seen, Hod is all about thoughts, so Netzach and Hod are thoughts and feelings in balance. Consider Netzach to be worlds of fairy magic, of sprites and woodland beings, as compared to Hod, where more scholarly pursuits feed the magic of the Tree and of you. However, those scholarly pursuits are undertaken with the understanding of the beautiful images produced by the artists of Netzach, as one feeds the other.

Have you every gazed at a piece of art and been lost in it, seeing precisely how the artist must have been feeling? Look at that statement again. You're seeing with your eyes, but you're feeling with your heart, using the Earthly sense of sight and yet feeling it stir your soul. That is Netzach, that feeling. Hod comes in when the art critic takes what you're feeling, explains what the artist is saying and quantifies it with clever words. A feeling turns into a conversation.

So, art and music are represented in Netzach. This Sephira is the inspiration for many people involved in these pursuits and home to spiritual guides with an interest in helping you make the most of your own talents. Visiting Netzach can help clear the way if you're feeling blocked in an artistic project.

In Netzach you'll also see the beginning of the lower self, the triangle of personality fed from Tiphareth, the last Sephira of the realms of the soul. Netzach, Hod, Yesod and Malkuth show themselves more in our lives because they work directly with the personality, but make no mistake, all the Sephiroth above them are there when you know where to look and how they present themselves!

The planetary ruler of Netzach is Venus, who needs no introduction – the planet of love, and love in all its forms, from family to partners and all points in between. But jealousy, anger and even hate sit here too, as Netzach plays host to all the feelings we have within us and express through our emotions.

These are balanced by Hod, which gives form to the force of Netzach. Think of a time when you were incandescent with rage, a strong and powerful force, then remember how you tempered that with a response that was more effective by being in a particular form – an eloquent letter of complaint, for example. Netzach to Hod to Yesod to Malkuth.

The balancing act of Hod and Netzach isn't always an easy one to keep up, though, and if anything's going to be heavily weighted, it's usually the side that looks at the feelings.

Victory over feelings

The word 'Victory' is used to describe Netzach, and it may seem an odd choice. Victory can bring images of banners waving, a war won, and perhaps that's not what you'd think of when considering the planet or goddess Venus. However, this isn't about victory over another individual, country or warring faction, it's victory over your feelings.

That isn't the same as being a cold fish; it means that when you have feelings that can seem overwhelming, you know what to do to bring them under control. You visit Hod and all its images and remind yourself that logic has its place, you think about what you're feeling, consider whether it's your stuff or not, and then if it is, you figure out how you can deal with it all. And when all that's done, you push it all out through Yesod.

Victory over feelings also means seeing love, beauty and perhaps the divine in everything, even in the most extreme circumstances. It's very, very difficult to imagine how that could be done if you were in a horrendous situation, perhaps being held hostage or imprisoned. How could you feel love, an appreciation for the divine, then? Here's a quote that helps to understand it a little more:

> *'I learned that courage was not the absence of fear, but the triumph over it. The brave man is not he who does not feel afraid, but he who conquers that fear.'*
> NELSON MANDELA

Victory over feelings.

However, consider this: in your many lives on Earth you will have faced challenging circumstances, situations you won't have to endure again, but someone you know may be going through tough times, even as you read this book. Your love and compassion for them come from the love and lessons you've learned on your own journey, perhaps from this life or perhaps from past lives. It is through love that we bring more love into this world of ours, through the divine nature of universal love found in the garden of Netzach.

The raw power of Netzach is one of creativity, of passion and of drive to bring down this most magnificent expression of the divine that is already within you, but what happens when you do that to the exclusion of all else? Perhaps you end up in your studio furiously chucking paint around, expressing your unbridled emotional self, and the lights go off or your partner leaves you because you've not paid the bill or bothered to acknowledge their existence in weeks. It is Hod that brings balance, logic that tells you that other things must co-exist alongside your passions in life.

Creatures of nature

We are creatures of nature and need it around us to bring balance into our world, a task Mother Nature struggles with in current times, but observe how nature truly works. Red in tooth and claw? There are few souls who aren't touched by the sight of a lioness feeding her cubs – apart from the mother of the gazelle that was her prey perhaps? But we accept it – it's nature. And then we can't accept a weed in our garden or a bug in the kitchen?

Animals don't stop to think or analyse; they do what they do. You are already beautiful, as perfect as that lioness, and you can do what you've incarnated to do if only you'll listen to the truth of your feelings and unselfishly give yourself to the whole being that you are.

Netzach is where your personality meets your soul, remember. Perhaps that's the heart of the matter?

Exercise: Expressing your inner Netzach

When you were little and you brought home a picture you'd painted – something lovely I'm sure – perhaps you gave it to your parents, who then gave it pride of place on the fridge door. It was an expression of your feelings as well as how you saw the world – through the eyes of a child, because you were one. Were you more emotional then, more in touch with your feelings perhaps? Is that child still there? Of course! So, grab some paints, some coloured crayons or pens, take a piece of blank paper and let those feelings out.

'But what shall I paint?' That's a question from someone who has Hod telling them they need form, they need instructions, permission perhaps. Really, you don't. Here's what you do:

❖ Take a deep breath, start with a colour or a doodle, start wherever you feel like starting and go for it! If you need help, find a younger member of the family and let them show you how it's done. Eat chocolate and ice-cream as you go, if it helps.

❖ When you've finished, put it on the fridge!

Sometimes our feelings need to be shaped into words, sometimes not so much.

Whilst writing this chapter, I thought about how indigenous people of many countries have lived with and as part of nature. Some still do, be they Native Americans, Australian Aborigines, the Ainu of Japan or many others. Much can be learned from them, or maybe a better way of putting it is to say the rest of us could do with unlearning things.

Angels

The archangel of Netzach is Haniel, Grace of God. She is beautiful, dressed like a Grecian goddess and has emeralds on her wingtips, as far as I can see! She reminds you that peace, beauty, grace and charm can go a very long way, but make no mistake, she is also aware of the laws of nature and she encourages you to bare your teeth, should the need arise. Not always a popular view when it comes to angels, yet Michael can take a sword and run it through a serpent, the symbol for knowledge. Go figure.

The angelic order is the Elohim, the rulers of nature, who whisper to every flower to bloom, much as they do to you too.

Vices and virtues

The vice of Netzach is unchastity and lust, but don't be misled by this: it's talking about lust for power for power's sake. Think about a relationship where one partner seeks to control the other – will that last? This also reminds you to maintain your own integrity and to love with all that love implies, to love unconditionally without seeking to fulfil your own agenda and lust after that alone.

Also consider the lust for power that's wrapped up in beauty, wrapped in pretty ribbons and promises of perfection that may never be delivered. In the modern world this particular vice is everywhere – the illusion of glamour, of being glamoured. That's not to say glamour is a bad thing. To be clear, for beauty's sake it's a wonderful thing, but used to profess, use or abuse power, it most certainly isn't. When you see the reality of the portrait, Dorian Gray is no longer appealing.

The virtue of Netzach is unselfishness. Kind of speaks for itself, really. If you can approach life knowing you neither own nor have any control over any sentient being, nature in all her glory and power or any archangel, sprite or elemental, then you have the virtue of Netzach within you. It's all about co-operation and mutual respect.

Tarot cards

The four sevens show us the challenges in life that are brought about through a battle within – through our feelings, challenging us to bring forward their truth – not by playing lip service to how we think we should feel, but admitting how we *really* feel.

- *Seven of Wands:* Lord of Valour. Feeling the fear and doing it anyway! Have courage in the face of the task ahead and believe in yourself.

- *Seven of Cups:* Lord of Debauch. That way temptation lies, and lust for gain with no thought for others. Stay true to your beliefs.

- *Seven of Swords:* Lord of Futility. No matter what you do, it won't make any difference, right? Not true. Break free by making a difference!

- *Seven of Disks:* Lord of Failure. You get back what you put in, so put in more and get more back! Resist negative self-talk.

Visiting Netzach

Before you embark upon the Netzach temple working, perhaps some time in nature would be a good idea. Go to your favourite place. Walk, sit by the ocean, stand under the trees in a forest, sit on the sand, take a wander around your garden and smell the flowers, literally! Set the tone.

Correspondences

- *Keyword:* Victory

- *Number:* Seven

- *Archangel:* Haniel

- *Order of angels:* Elohim

- *Planet:* Venus

- *Virtue:* Unselfishness

- *Vice:* Lust for power

- *Gods/goddesses:* Aphrodite, Hathor, Lakshmi, Venus

- *Colour:* Green

- *Crystals:* Emerald, rose quartz, tourmaline

- *Incense:* Rose

- *Body parts:* Hip area, loins

- *Tarot cards:* The sevens

Exercise: The Temple of Netzach

Prepare in your usual way and pay particular attention to your altar. It's always beautiful, I'm sure, but really go for it with Netzach – let your creativity flow, get those roses out.

Perform your protection and energy work. Create your sacred and beautiful space according to your own divine creativity.

Ask your guides, Archangel Haniel and the divine beings of Netzach to assist you.

Use your 4-2-4-2 breathing or any technique you're comfortable with to count yourself down into a meditative state of being.

❖ Allow the material world to melt away and replace it with the temple forest. See it, feel it, be in it completely.

❖ Once you're in the garden, perhaps already in the clearing, see your Tree. This time it will be an emerald that breaks free from the shifting, sparkling green of the Tree of Life.

❖ As it forms a green sphere in front of you, walk towards it, considering what Netzach means to you. What nature, love or artistic story do you carry with you?

❖ Project the symbol for Venus onto the sphere as you walk into it and through into the garden of Netzach.

❖ You find yourself in a beautiful rose garden, white walled and full of statues of Greek and Roman gods and goddesses. Which ones do you recognize?

❖ Pause a moment, look at the symbols around you, remember all of them and be aware of your feelings in this realm.

❖ Feel the creative part of your soul sing. Listen to the song and feel the urge to be creative that sits in all of us.

❖ Talk with any creatures who fly, crawl or walk your way. They can communicate here. They can on Earth, too, if you take the time to listen, but remember this is the land of feelings, so feel their energy, their mood and their message.

❖ Walk with beauty, walk with grace, walk in the perfection that you already are and see how everyone and everything else is doing the same. Feel that. Feel it in every fibre of your being, recognize it!

❖ You may see a Grecian temple ahead of you, with two great leopards guarding the entrance, or a simple clearing with seven stones marking a boundary.

❖ You see Aphrodite exit and walk towards you, then you realize it's Haniel, archangel of Netzach. What does your Haniel look like?

❖ Commune with Haniel or any other beings in this place of feelings, colour, music and art. Ask for guidance on how to use the virtue of Netzach and avoid the vice, avoid being glamoured.

❖ And now ask for a vision of victory that you can use in your own life in the here and now.

❖ When you have finished communing with your hosts, they may offer you a gift, a reminder of your visit to these realms. Return their kindness with a promise made to work with and respect the power of this Sephira in your own life and on your own Tree.

❖ It's time for you to leave. Walk back along the path to the emerald sphere, feeling that information you've collected sink in.

❖ Surround yourself in the emerald green that takes you back to the temple forest in the realms of Malkuth.

❖ Bring your awareness back to your surroundings, and when you're ready, close your meditation.

Make notes, take a Tarot card and remember to eat and drink!

Netzach consolidation

'The real magic is in making the intangible idea, the creative impulse, manifest and live in our reality.'
Mark Ryan, actor

'I have a dream...'
Remind yourself of the dream you stated in Malkuth.

Astrology
Where is Venus in you chart? What aspects can you find around her and what does it tell you about the way you love?

Tarot cards
❖ Going into the temple: Card

❖ Coming out of the temple: Card

❖ Consolidating the temple: Card

The route the cards are taking
A short analysis of what the cards tell you.

Analysis of the temple visualization
How you felt, what you saw, what the symbols mean to you.

How it has manifested in your life
How has it presented itself in your life here on Earth? What have you noticed that you missed before? What do you want to change?

'Moving forward, I commit to...'
Make a commitment to making those changes happen.

The personality triangle

Let's put it all together. Tightening up what you've learned along the way is an important discipline to follow. Take it from someone who tried the other approach. It helps you better understand where you are now as well as how far you've come.

A consolidation would normally occur after each pathworking, but as this is an introduction I'm giving you, it's going to take place after each set of three Sephiroth, too. Why these three – Yesod, Hod and Netzach? Because they form the personality triangle.

Getting personal

The beauty of Qabalah is that it brings its lessons into real life. It sits in front of you, reminding you that it's real, not something you simply read about and ponder. Bearing that in mind, it's time to review the events of the past few weeks or months.

The personality triangle consolidation

'I have a dream...'
What is your dream, your goal?

Looking at each Sephira, how has it been reflected in your life?

❖ *Yesod:* Cycles

❖ *Hod:* Thoughts

❖ *Netzach:* Feelings

Astrology

Look at the position of the Moon, Mercury and Venus in your chart. What information do they give you?

Tarot cards

Put the following cards on a table in their relevant positions:

❖ The Tower horizontally

❖ The Sun at a 45-degree angle on the left

❖ The Star at a 45-degree angle on the right

The route the cards are taking

Look at the cards, analyse them and think about how they might work with the Sephiroth and in your life. Remember the example of The Tower card running between your thoughts and feelings.

What does this tell you about your personality?

Are there cycles you could do without?

Are there those in your life who need to know how you truly feel? Or perhaps you need to slow down to listen to them?

'I have learned...'

Ask questions, let your intuition flow. Think, *Planets, Sephiroth, cards, images, meditations, experiences,* and put it all together to come up with a statement that begins:

From the personality triangle I have learned...

To help you finish this section, here's a meditation you can do when you've finished your consolidation.

Exercise: Vision of the personality triangle

Perform the Qabalistic Cross (*see page 66*) and prepare in the usual way.

Sit down, relax and close your eyes, begin to breathe 4-2-4-2.

❖ Allow the material world to melt away and make your way to your forest, to the clearing and into the tree.

❖ Sandalphon is waiting for you. He guides you to the pillars. Stand in front of them, ebony on your left, ivory on your right.

❖ As you face the pillars, you see that a curtain, a thin veil, is hanging between them.

❖ Sandalphon asks you to look through the veil.

❖ At first you see nothing, but as you concentrate, you begin to see a violet light. It is misty at first, but then it seems to be alive with colour.

❖ Then an image appears, of a Chinese pagoda, its roof made of silver with mother of pearl in its walls: the temple of Yesod.

❖ The garden has a lake with a half-moon bridge across it. The Moon itself is reflected in the water. Is it full, new, waxing or waning?

❖ Gabriel stands in the garden smiling at you, sending love.

❖ The image fades and an orange light appears, again misty but soon clearing.

❖ As it disappears you see a frozen wasteland, a blank canvas.

❖ Rumbling up through the ice comes the ice temple of Hod, created from your thoughts, as all things are created.

❖ Frozen into its walls are the major arcana of the Tarot. Does one card stand out for you more than any other?

❖   Raphael stands looking at you. Make his image as clear as you can.

❖   This image fades and you begin to see an emerald green light. As its brightness wanes, a lush landscape appears, with rolling green hills and flowers in abundance, and colours such as you've never seen before.

❖   On a hill in the distance you will see a Grecian temple. Outside are two leopards guarding its entrance.

❖   Below the temple is a rose garden. The garden has many statues of Greek and Roman gods and goddesses.

❖   Haniel smiles and sends love and peace to you.

❖   Let this fade now and bring your attention back to the veil and to Malkuth.

❖   Sandalphon leads you back from the pillars. Thank him for your time here.

❖   He acknowledges you and says it's time to leave.

❖   Move into the clearing and into the forest.

❖   Bring your awareness back into the room you're in.

Make notes and, when you're ready, have something to eat and drink. Take a Tarot card.

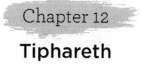

Chapter 12

Tiphareth

This Sephira sits in the centre of the tree and is the balancing point. It's where we first encounter the energy of the soul on the climb up from Malkuth. Of course, that also means it's where the soul gives way for the personality on the way down!

Tiphareth sits on the pillar of equilibrium, the Middle Pillar, the middle way. This Sephira is a child to Kether, a king in Malkuth, and in its role as the Sephira of transmutation it's where we meet the sacrificed gods, all those, from Odin to Christ, who give so that others can benefit. It's where we meet the God-force incarnate, the gods who meet an untimely sacrificial end to take the karmic conditions, pain and troubles from humanity, and it's where they also rise again.

Here you're asked what you're prepared to give up to fulfil your higher calling, to take responsibility for yourself rather than expect others to do it for you.

The four Sephira below, Netzach, Hod, Yesod and Malkuth, have shown you the personality issues you are encountering.

Now it's time to embark upon the journey to the higher self by placing yourself in Tiphareth and making a connection with your soul by formally acknowledging its presence and clearing your vision and hearing so you can take onboard the messages from your true will.

Are you ready? This is your own inner voice speaking. It's not guides or astral beings, it's not the direction of anyone other than your own higher self, your own soul, and it's very important to remember that. Thy will be done.

This balancing-point is one of my favourite Sephira. It's very, very special to me and I hope it will be to you. As you look at the Tree, you can see that it can be entirely turned around on this axis, so it's not only about balancing severity and mercy, but about balancing lower and higher Sephiroth, too. What a magnificent piece of design!

If you consider what's happening here, you could see it as the point of incarnation, as this is where the soul joins the personality. Even though the path, the Universe path, from Yesod to Malkuth, is sometimes seen as that point, perhaps it's easier to consider that as physical birth and this as the acceptance of the soul – its agreement to come into this world with all it has learned from its many lives and karmic conditions, and its divinity, grace, understanding and wisdom. In Tiphareth you will find your shining self, your higher self, the mediator between the higher realms and yourself, all in the title!

Ego can step in here, with the assumption that you are now a mighty being of power and glory and can command the lower realms to manifest anything you desire. If it's solely about what *you* desire, it's ego. The higher self is concerned with the harmony and wellbeing of *others*, even if that means sacrifice. The vice of Tiphareth, as we'll see later, is false pride.

The higher realms

As you climb the Tree, you'll feel the difference in the higher realms. This is where you really do get that first initiation into a great shift in your energy. Sometimes this can test friendships, amongst other things. It's something I experienced and choices had to be made. If you encounter it, you must do what you feel is right.

This is the Sephira associated with the Christ energy and perhaps that may be uncomfortable for some, but every faith is represented on the Tree, as it recognizes the simple fact that they are all from the same source. Some faiths identify more with Kether, some with Yesod, while others look to the green worlds of Netzach for the beauty of Earth magic, Wicca and paganism.

This is also the Sephira of illumination, where you see the glory of the upper realms and your conscious mind catches images of the truth of your soul and how magnificently beautiful it is. It's where you are crowned as having sought out the truth of your soul and found it, and believe me when I say the light within you changes.

You also begin to understand your own energy more, how perhaps it's depleted because you're not getting back as much as you put in and, as odd as it may seem in such a sacred space, that could also be highlighted through the exchange of gold, through money, which is an energy of course. There must be fair exchange and Tiphareth can highlight where there is not.

It's a place of great healing, of love and also of sacrifice, for what greater love can you show for another than giving something up so that they can blossom? It's not a pre-requisite, before you panic; it's simply that soul energy is usually experienced in the act of helping others, be that sacrificial or not. Who or what would you sacrifice everything for?

The keyword, 'Beauty', reminds you there is beauty in everything if you look for it. Sometimes you do have to look very hard, but it's there, and in seeing it, you will have reflected it back into even the darkest heart.

You may have heard the expression 'soul decision'. This is where those are made, and seeing the beauty in everything is what will help you make them.

This is also a place where your soul learns from those who have gone before. You may experience the feeling that 'someone' is watching over you or that a specific piece of knowledge is being put your way. Teachers often appear, both Earthly and spiritual.

Angels

The archangel is Raphael, but sometimes people see Michael too. Raphael is renowned for his healing qualities, so it makes sense that he is here, and of course the fiery Michael suits the element of Fire in this temple. Michael is also a healer; he deals more with deep-rooted injury than Raphael. In the upcoming meditation you will see Raphael, but trust and if you see Michael, then so be it!

The angelic force of Tiphareth is the Malachim, the kings. Amongst other things, they are seen as the great elemental kings you met in Malkuth on a higher level, as keepers of the balance between the solar systems of the universe. Perhaps they also balance the worlds of the higher Sephiroth with those of the lower?

Astrology

The Sun governs Tiphareth and it's easy to link this planet, strictly speaking a luminary, with the experience of this Sephira. Here you are reaching for your higher good, the part of you that wants to act from as high a level as you can, and when the Sun shines down on you, you feel good. When you act from your soul level, you feel great!

This balancing-point is a wonderful space to be in. When was the last time you felt so balanced?

Vices and virtues

The vice of Tiphareth is false pride. You've already seen that it has its roots in ego. There's nothing wrong with taking pride in your work and what you've achieved – you absolutely should – but in attaining great things, you should also share great things. Energy exchange means giving and receiving in balance.

The virtue is devotion to the Great Work – reaching for something higher, and helping others do the same perhaps? For me, this devotion, this virtue, is something that burns in my chest when it needs to remind me to take the higher road. What's right may not be what your personality or ego wants to hear, but there you have it!

Tarot cards

The Tarot cards are the four sixes:

- *Six of Wands:* Lord of Victory. Having passed through a tough training course, you have gained a victory, reached a point of ascension.

- *Six of Cups:* Lord of Pleasure. Entering into pleasure with an open heart, you are willing to receive the blessings ahead.

- *Six of Swords:* Lord of Science. Clarity comes to a difficult decision, as you now see things clearly.

- *Six of Disks:* Lord of Success. Abundance comes to you – more than you need, so remember to pass some on.

Visiting Tiphareth

To help you when you visit Tiphareth, find a way to balance your chakra system other than through the meditation (*page 67*). You can find chakra balancings through crystal energy, colour energy or perhaps sound therapy? For me sound therapy is astounding, for others not so much. Find what works for you.

Correspondences

- Keyword: Beauty
- Number: Six
- Archangel(s): Raphael/Michael
- Order of angels: Malachim
- Planet: The Sun
- Virtue: Devotion to the Great Work

- Vice: False pride
- Gods/goddesses: Adonis, Apollo, Helios, Krishna, Ra, Vishnu
- Colour: Yellow
- Crystals: Citrine, topaz, yellow diamond
- Incense: Frankincense
- Body part: Breast
- Tarot cards: The sixes

Exercise: The Temple of Tiphareth

Don't forget to dress your altar and to use the incense associated with this Sephira, frankincense. Take a Tarot card before your meditation.

Perform your protection and energy work. Create your sacred and beautiful space according to your own divine creativity.

Ask your guides, Archangel Raphael or Michael and the divine beings of Tiphareth to assist you.

Use your 4-2-4-2 breathing or any technique you're comfortable with to count yourself down into a meditative state of being.

- ❖ Allow the material world to melt away and replace it with the temple forest. See it, feel it, be in it completely.

- ❖ Once you're in the garden, in the clearing, see your Tree. This time it will be a citrine crystal that breaks free from the shifting, sparkling branches of the Tree of Life.

- ❖ As you stand in the garden, consider your thoughts on Tiphareth, on sacrifice for the good of others, on what it means to work with your higher self and how to bring all that into your life.

❖ The citrine will spin until it stands before you as a ball of yellow light tinged with golden flecks. Use the symbol for the Sun to enter the sphere.

❖ As you do so, you feel radiant yourself, full of that beautiful golden light.

❖ Feel balanced, at peace. Walk forward, communing with any beings that come your way in this, your Tiphareth experience.

❖ As you reach the garden of Tiphareth, you will see the temple. Perhaps it's a great cathedral, perhaps it's a six-sided open-air temple of simple beauty?

❖ From the temple, your chosen archangel, Michael or Raphael, comes towards you. He has a message for you. You may also see one of the many sacrificed gods, a child, a king or a majestic lion.

❖ Ask them how you can use the energy of Tiphareth in your life in the here and now for the highest good of others and yourself. How can you use sacrifice, harmony and balance?

❖ Feel the golden radiance of this space and the beings here. Now see how you too are vibrating with that energy.

❖ You will be offered a gift and in return you offer yours; a commitment to use the energy of Tiphareth through its virtue of devotion to the Great Work and to avoid its vice, false pride.

❖ When you're ready, return to the yellow citrine sphere and back into the temple forest and watch as the citrine returns to the Tree.

❖ Return to your normal surroundings and close your meditation down.

Make notes in preparation for your consolidation of Tiphareth and when you're ready eat and drink. Take a Tarot card.

Tiphareth consoliation

'The important thing is this: to be able, at any moment, to sacrifice what we are for what we could become.'
MAHARISHI MAHESH YOGI

'I have a dream...'
Remind yourself of the dream you stated in Malkuth.

Astrology
Look at the Sun in your chart. What does it tell you about your will? Look at the position, sign and aspects.

Tarot cards
❖ Going into the temple: Card

❖ Coming out of the temple: Card

❖ Consolidating the temple: Card

The route the cards are taking
A short analysis of what the cards tell you.

Analysis of the temple visualization
How you felt, what you saw, what the symbols mean to you.

How it has manifested in your life
How has it presented itself in your life here on Earth? What have you noticed that you missed before? What do you want to change?

Moving forward, I commit to...'
Make a commitment to making those changes happen.

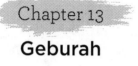

Chapter 13

Geburah

The ruby red sphere of Geburah has many a group or individual wondering just what karma has in store for them, but Geburah isn't punitive, it's a cleansing process. Here you recognize just what has to happen to help you move on. Remember you're in the land of the soul's journey, so maybe some of the decisions won't sit comfortably with the personality, but your soul knows what's right and it's been my experience that the personality knows when the soul's right, too!

This Sephira has always been one I approach with extra respect and reverence, just as you would any burning fire or molten lava flow! Recognizing when you're in Geburah isn't easy sometimes, as anger clouds your vision red, but the simplest answer is already obvious: you're in it when you can't see for anger and frustration.

This Sephira is one that many initiates into the Tree of Life worry about. It fills them with dread, but that really isn't necessary. You can have a tough time in any of the Sephiroth, and in the world of opposites you can have a great time in any of the Sephiroth as well, and that includes Geburah.

Geburah teaches you that what you fear may be the very thing that makes you stronger, makes you wiser and makes you get off your backside and do something about changing things in your life.

When things have run their course, when you just don't know why you're plodding on, there is Geburah, ready to cut the ties that bind. But it always leaves things healed, dealt with properly rather than left unresolved, waiting to gather the moss of karmic debt because you just didn't sort everything out before moving on.

Karma is neither negative nor positive; it simply is. It's a reaction to decisions you – and only you – have made. Accepting that responsibility will help you work with this highly effective Sephira.

This is also home to the Lords of Karma, beings who have an interest in what you create and negate. They also have the bigger plan, your soul's plan, as well as that of the universal state of the nations they govern.

Geburah is one up from Hod on the Pillar of Severity, and where Hod is your individual thoughts, Geburah is the power to make them happen as your soul puts on its personal trainer's hat and urges you on. Geburah can destroy what no longer serves you well, but all in the name of elevating you and bringing your will into being, just as you have stated in Tiphareth, just as you now identify with.

Of course, left unattended, the power of Geburah can be overdone, but remember that no Sephira operates on its own and, as ever, the Tree of Life has its balancing-points. For Geburah, that is Chesed, home to the Lords of Peace. A carrot and stick approach, but which situation requires which Sephira?

Imagine a chariot race. You have one red horse and one blue horse, one for Geburah and one for Chesed. In order to stay the course, to steer the course, you must fire up the power of the red one whilst using the sensibilities of the blue one. You must know when to ask for more power and when to pull it back and ask for a steadier, gentler pace.

It's also important to remember that the power of Geburah isn't personal. Changes that occur under its influence shouldn't been seen as punishment, ever. Whilst some of these changes can be traumatic, they bring the chance of new beginnings, just like our friend the phoenix rising from the flames renewed, better, stronger and ready for new challenges. Consider the catastrophe of natural disasters and the rebuilding of what has been destroyed. You don't replace like with like, you replace it with better, as a result of lessons learned.

This Sephira reminds you that not everything is sugar-coated and covered in glitter. Like you need reminding, but some spiritual practices assume change is as simple as willing it to be different. The will of the personality may not be in line with the will of soul, however, based on karmic lessons and deep truths that must be uncovered to advance the soul's knowledge.

As you stand amid ashes, surrounded by charred remains of what you thought was the truth, left disappointed but still able to see the merit in the moment, you will understand the real strength of this Sephira. Dusting yourself off, accepting what has happened and spreading your newly tempered wings and committing to building stronger, higher and better than ever before – that's Geburah.

Angels

Khamael is the archangel of Geburah. Strong and courageous, he is the archangel of justice. He will test your convictions, ask you to show your true intentions and purify your thoughts through acceptance of the consequences of your actions. He also tempers the energy of the lightning flash as it descends the Tree, adding more when needed, holding back when it's not. Karma in motion.

Take care to act the same way. If you assume that this power is yours to wield any way you see fit, you might just discover that things don't go according to plan. Over-use of Geburah can sometimes lead to destructive forces being unleashed. Consider the consequences of your actions – that way, Geburah and karma go hand in hand.

The angelic order of Geburah is the Seraphim, the burning ones, carrying destructive power and the ability to purify, to take away that which is not part of the vision of perfection.

Vices and virtues

The vice is cruelty – cruelty that destroys what you or other have created, cruelty for cruelty's sake.

The virtue is courage – the courage to act or speak up when others won't, to let your soul lead and to be creative. Yes, often that takes courage, too.

Tarot cards

The number five in Tarot is often seen as trouble, a bothersome influence that demands you take some action. It can of course mean you're releasing such energy and coming to terms with the root of the bother, but when the fives appear, think *Geburah*, think *What can I do to move things along? What needs to be faced and what may need cutting away?*

- *Five of Wands:* Lord of Strife. Restrictions, frustration. Find a way to work through what may be a difficult time. Use humour perhaps?

- *Five of Cups:* Lord of Disappointment. Someone is going to let you down, make you feel a bit fed up. Accept it or move on.

- *Five of Swords:* Lord of Defeat. Your hopes may be dented, but don't let this affect every aspect of your life. See the lessons within.

- *Five of Disks:* Lord of Worry. The future may look gloomy, but making it look gloomier won't help. Change what you can, accept what you can't.

To remove something that's hanging on and being an unnecessary drag on your progress, try this cutting the cord exercise. Please be sure this is the message you want to send before proceeding, though. You don't have to proceed – there is no 'have to' here.

Exercise: Cutting the cord

Perform the Qabalistic Cross (*see page 66*).

Get ready to meditate, or just contemplate if that's your way.

❖ Visualize the situation you're attached to. See a cord running between you and that situation. Some see it as a sparkly silver rope.

❖ How thick is the bond? Obviously if it's very thick, it may take longer to cut than a wispy cord.

❖ How sparkly is it – or maybe it's not sparkly at all? Does it form a chain, is it silken? What does the appearance of the cord tell you about this situation?

❖ Recognize this wasn't forced on you – you played your part in its forming.

❖ Spend a moment thanking the energy this cord has brought you. No doubt lessons have been learned and routes for the future will be clearer.

❖ Now cut the cord. Snap it if you can. Or use whatever you see – it may be scissors, or even industrial cutters, if you need them!

❖ The space must now be filled with love. Seal the area with white or pink light. Seal your auric body.

❖ Come back to your usual awareness. Record your images and how you felt.

It's not uncommon for any folks involved in the other end of your cord to feel something as well as you. They might even get in touch to try to reconnect with you. Only you can decide yay or nay!

Visiting Geburah

Correspondences

* *Keywords:* Severity/Strength

* *Number:* Five

* *Archangel:* Khamael

* *Order of angels:* Seraphim

* *Planet:* Mars

* *Virtue:* Courage, energy

* *Vice:* Cruelty, destruction

* *Gods/goddesses:* Aries, Athena, Kali, Mars, Morrighan, Sekhmet

* *Colour:* Red

* *Crystals:* Bloodstone, red carnelian, ruby

* *Incense:* Tobacco

* *Body part:* Right arm

* *Tarot cards:* The fives

Exercise: The Temple of Geburah

Perform your protection and energy work. Create your sacred and beautiful space according to your own divine creativity.

Ask your guides, Archangel Khamael and the divine beings of Geburah to assist you.

Use your 4-2-4-2 breathing or any technique you're comfortable with to count yourself down into a meditative state of being.

❖ Allow the material world to melt away and replace it with the temple forest. See it, feel it, be in it completely.

❖ Once you're in the garden, perhaps already in the clearing, see your Tree. This time it will be a ruby that breaks free from the shifting, sparkling branches of the Tree of Life.

❖ As it forms a red sphere in front of you, walk towards it, considering what Geburah means to you and where you need to be more forceful, courageous even.

❖ Project the symbol for Mars onto the sphere as you walk into it and through into the red worlds and garden of Geburah.

❖ Consider the lessons and gifts of Geburah and how you could use them. What's relevant to you right here, right now?

❖ Feel the heat as you walk through, smell the smoke and imagine the power, strength and courage flowing through your body.

❖ In this realm, the beings may challenge you, confront you, push some of your buttons, all in the name of exposing what makes you frustrated or angry.

❖ Look at why, look at who, look at the choices you have. How you respond is your karma.

❖ The heat is oppressive; it can slow you down, just as feeling anger without making good use of it will slow you down.

❖ The temple of Geburah in the distance can be seen as a solid ruby building with black iron gates and windows. Is it a fortress? A castle? Perhaps it's a blazing fire surrounded by five stone seats waiting for you to commune with your guides?

❖ Walk through the steamy, red hot garden of Geburah towards the temple.

❖ The archangel of Geburah, Khamael, comes towards you, mighty and powerful. How does your Khamael look?

❖ Ask him for a vision of power – how that looks to you on your path right now, how it shows itself in your life, how you can use it. Ask with confidence. See it, feel it.

❖ Commune further with Khamael and as he offers you a gift, offer him one in the form of your commitment to pay more attention to how you wield your own power.

❖ When you're ready, follow the path back through the hot and steamy garden of Geburah back to that ruby light.

❖ Say your farewells, pay any further respects and walk into the ruby light and back into the temple forest of Malkuth.

❖ Allow the forest to fade and return to your usual surroundings.

When you have closed your meditation down, take a Tarot card, make notes and remember to eat and drink something. No matter how small, it's symbolic of grounding your energy here on Earth.

Geburah consolidation

'Karma, when properly understood, is just the mechanics through which consciousness manifests.'

DEEPAK CHOPRA

'I have a dream...'

Remind yourself of the dream you stated in Malkuth.

Astrology

Look at Mars in your chart, his placement and the aspects, and ask where you feel you need to do some editing!

Tarot cards

❖ Going into the temple: Card

❖ Coming out of the temple: Card

❖ Consolidating the temple: Card

The route the cards are taking

A short analysis of what the cards tell you.

Analysis of the temple visualization

How you felt, what you saw, what the symbols mean to you.

How it has manifested in your life

How has it presented itself in your life here on Earth? What have you noticed that you missed before? What do you want to change?

'Moving forward, I commit to...'

Make a commitment to making those changes happen.

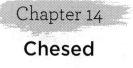

Chapter 14

Chesed

Chesed is the balance to Geburah. It's home to the Lords of Peace, who encourage growth, help you expand your world view and balance severity with mercy – war with peace. It sits above Netzach on the Pillar of Mercy, reminding us that whilst the love found in the realms of Venus and Netzach is passionate, there is also the love of a father for his child, a guiding energy that has been there, done that and wants to share the wisdom.

When you imagine your next big project, see it in your mind's eye – how it will look, what colours you will use, who will use it or read it, what impact it may have, how it will come into being and beyond – that is Chesed. You're forming your kingdom, building those images on a higher plane, ready for Geburah and the editing process, ready for it to be balanced in Tiphareth, coloured in in Netzach, given words in Hod and passed to Yesod for the great machinery of the universe to make it so and bring it to birth in Malkuth.

This Sephira is often seen as the gift-giver. Indeed, on my own journey on the Tree of Life we were asked to request a gift as we reached the Temple of Chesed, to ask for whatever we desired. Never one to pass up an opportunity, I asked for a house. Why not? I didn't want a free one, I was happy to work for it, and the truth is, what I wanted was my own space, somewhere to call home, as I was renting a room at the time.

I was working as a deputy manager in a small hotel and not making much money, but I achieved it. I got my house, along with a 100 per cent mortgage, which at the time was rare, but the mortgage adviser, whom I had never met, trusted me and to date I have never let her down! I'm not sharing this so that Chesed becomes a place for to you ask for stuff, but to show you that the power of the Tree of Life is in the everyday as much as in the extraordinary. Make no mistake, if you visit Chesed to ask for stuff, you will get it, but Chesed will demand payment in some way or other. As for my gift, even though a house seems very *personality* based, rather than spiritual, the space, peace and tranquillity it brought my *soul* was the true gift.

As the first Sephira below the upper triangle of Kether, Chokmah and Binah, Chesed will bring form to what you will soon see are increasingly abstract ideas. It holds within it the highest ideals, the concept of royalty at its most noble and magnificent. It's the king on the throne of a kingdom at peace as opposed to the king in a chariot ready for war, as depicted in Geburah. When you feel frustrated by your emotional responses, annoyed at what he said or she said, worried about what might happen next, think of Chesed. Here you meet that part of yourself that rises above it all.

If you were royalty, you'd surely want to rule with a guiding hand that was merciful and benevolent, perhaps like a parent keeping the family on the straight and narrow. This Sephira reminds us that we have a role to play in the lives of others as well as in our own. It encourages us to be all that we can be. Obedience here is obedience to your soul and your spiritual values.

This is also the home of the Masters, a term that's used all too loosely these days, with many claiming to be Masters of this, that or the other. In this context, the Masters are disincarnate beings who oversee groups of souls and individuals therein, those who show the potential to reach higher realms of understanding and work with and within those realms. Philosophy, art and education are of interest to these Masters and they often take on large groups of people to help them on their path.

They are from humanity themselves; they are from our ranks. So they know what you're going through and will encourage you to keep going, trekking up the mountain to reach your goals.

When visiting Chesed, you may see Masters in the garden. Eventually one may speak to you or even take you under their guidance, but know that will not happen until you are truly ready. When it does, it is a compliment indeed.

The ability to control power is important here. That is probably true in all of the Sephiroth, as they are all powers, but in Chesed more so, for here you're asked to be careful what you manifest and to consider whether it's for the good of all, or only of yourself.

So much is made of abundance, of attraction, nowadays. In the modern world, it always seems to be about *stuff*. Stuff is great – but stuff isn't so great when others around literally have nothing to eat, nowhere to sleep and no country to call their own. Chesed seeks the higher ground; only when all of the kingdom is taken care of will the benevolent ruler rest. That is true abundance and the true use of the law of attraction.

Angels

Tzadkiel is the archangel of Chesed. He is associated with magic and the Masters who populate this Sephira. He is often seen as the angel of good luck too, but luck is earned as far as Tzadkiel is concerned. He reminds us to do the right thing. Sometimes that's not easy, but it has its rewards.

The angelic host are the Chashmalim, the brilliant or shining ones, the higher aspect of the Elohim in Netzach.

Astrology

Jupiter is the planetary force of Chesed. It's also the planet of your higher ideals, and as Chesed is about your soul values, you can see how it's perfectly placed. Jupiter aligns you with your higher self and of course when you are aligned, it seems that everything falls into place. Because it does.

Vices and virtues

The vices of Chesed are bigotry, hypocrisy, gluttony, tyranny. The danger of Chesed is feeling you're the only who's right, the only one who's on the true path, when in fact 'there are many roads to my father's castle'. Consider the less favourable facets of a religious organization that claims divine sovereignty and that it is doing the work of its chosen Master (for that's who Christ, Buddha and many others are, Masters), whilst sitting on hoards of money (energy) that could be dispersed to help those less fortunate. It's shown in spiritual circles, too, in jockeying for position and measuring worth with awards and 'who knows who' nonsense.

The virtue of Chesed is obedience – obedience to your higher self without assuming everyone wants to be told what to do and you're the one to do it! It's mercy given to all, not just those who think the same way as you do.

Tarot cards

The fours are cards that offer rewards. They are good news cards and when you see them, gifts are coming for a job well done. This is about receiving confirmation that you're on the right track, though, not about assuming that you've been good so you're owed a gift. That won't work!

- *Four of Wands:* Lord of Completion. The job may be done and well done, but what's next?

- *Four of Cups:* Lord of Luxury. Count your blessings, appreciate those who love you and love them right back!

- *Four of Swords:* Lord of Truce. Call a halt, take the higher ground and, after what may be some harsh words, find a way through.

- *Four of Disks:* Lord of Power. When you have achieved success, share it, be that financially or with advice. Keep it moving.

Exercise: Chesed awareness

To understand this Sephira better, try this exercise.

Be alone with your thoughts

Find some time where you can be alone with your thoughts. Look at your biases, the judgements you make in life, including the stuff that's hiding in the corners!

- ❖ Why do you feel the way you do?

- ❖ Is there something that's happened to you that could explain it, something that needs to be released into the fiery cleansing of Geburah?

- ❖ How can you move past it, towards a better way of being?

Start practising what you preach

- ❖ Treat others as you'd like to be treated yourself.

When you find yourself moaning about someone, ask why and whether it's worth it. Is it really that important and are they simply doing what they believe in, finding their own way through?

Acknowledge there may be another way and learn from it

You have two ears and one mouth for a reason: you're designed to listen. But remember that as you've reached the realms of Chesed, you're not only listening with those ears, but alos seeing from a new perspective. Use it.

Volunteer

Give something back. In doing so, you're working directly from your higher self and learning about other people's perspective, as well as opening yourself up to work with people who have hearts bigger than their desire for the latest smartphone. Always a good thing.

Visiting Chesed

Correspondences

- Keyword: Mercy

- Number: Four

- Archangel: Tzadkiel

- Order of angels: Chashmalim

- Planet: Jupiter

- Virtue: Obedience

- Vice: Bigotry, gluttony

- Gods/goddesses: Amon-Ra, Brahma, Indra, Jupiter, Thor, Zeus

- Colour: Blue

- Crystals: Amethyst, sapphire

- Incense: Cedar

- Body part: Left arm

- Tarot cards: The fours

Exercise: The Temple of Chesed

Decorate your altar. Cedar is the incense to use here and the rich sapphire blue of this beautiful Sephira will set the tone.

Don't forget to take a Tarot card before your meditation.

Perform your protection and energy work. Create your sacred and beautiful space according to your own divine creativity.

Ask your guides, Archangel Tzadkiel and the divine beings of Chesed to assist you.

Use your 4-2-4-2 breathing or any technique you're comfortable with to count yourself down into a meditative state of being.

❖ Allow the material world to melt away and replace it with the temple forest. See it, feel it, be in it completely. Use all your senses.

❖ Once you're in the temple garden, perhaps already in the clearing, see your Tree. This time it will be a sapphire that breaks free from the shifting, sparkling branches of the Tree of Life.

❖ As it forms a blue sphere in front of you, walk towards it, considering what Chesed means to you. Where do you need to bring peace and love into your life?

❖ Project the symbol for Jupiter onto the sphere as you walk into it and through into the blue world and garden of Chesed, a garden that appears to be high in the mountains amongst snow and rock.

❖ Consider the lessons and gifts of Chesed and how you could use them. What's relevant to you right here, right now?

❖ Feel yourself expand as you walk through, smell the cedar and imagine yourself a benevolent king or queen, much loved throughout your kingdom.

❖ In this realm the beings are generous with their knowledge. They know that in sharing it, change is made.

❖ The Temple of Chesed is sometimes seen as being made from blue sapphire. From the garden, you see its mighty door, inlaid with amethyst and gold. Or do you? How does your Chesed appear? Simpler perhaps? Mine certainly does!

❖ Tzadkiel, the archangel of Chesed, the mighty archangel of love and peace and good luck, comes towards you.

❖ Ask him for a vision of love, how it looks to you on your path right now, how it shows itself in your life. Ask with confidence for the opportunity to embrace your grand plans.

❖ Commune further with Tzadkiel and as he offers you a gift, offer him one in the form of your commitment to pay more attention to how you reward and encourage others and yourself.

❖ Do you see any Masters in the garden? If so, who?

❖ When you're ready, follow the path back through the snow and rock towards your blue sphere of light.

❖ Say your farewells, pay any further respects and walk into the blue light and back into the temple forest of Malkuth.

❖ Allow the forest to fade and return to your usual surroundings.

When you have closed your meditation down, take a Tarot card, make notes and remember to eat and drink something. No matter how small, it's symbolic of grounding your energy here on Earth.

Chesed consolidation

'One act of obedience is better than one hundred sermons.'
DIETRICH BONHOEFFER, THEOLOGIAN

'I have a dream...'
Remind yourself of the dream you stated in Malkuth.

Astrology
Look at Jupiter in your chart, his placement and aspects, and ask where obedience to your higher self shows itself and what you can do to honour it.

Tarot cards
❖ Going into the temple: Card

❖ Coming out of the temple: Card

❖ Consolidating the temple: Card

The route the cards are taking
A short analysis of what the cards tell you.

Analysis of the temple visualization
How you felt, what you saw, what the symbols mean to you.

How it has manifested in your life
How has it presented itself in your life here on Earth? What have you noticed that you missed before? What do you want to change?

'Moving forward, I commit to...'
Make a commitment to making those changes happen.

The soul triangle

The soul isn't perfect in and of itself – it's still fed by the spiritual triangle – but it's a long way up the Tree and is making decisions from higher energy as well as connecting to some highly evolved beings in order to help you.

Remember that everything will manifest eventually in Malkuth, so the purer your intention up the Tree, the purer the result at the bottom of it.

Your soul may have given you information that you're not so keen on – it could be challenging and perhaps hard work looms. But if you're coming at it from a point of truth and honesty with yourself, any changes will be matched by opportunities and balance will be restored.

The soul triangle consolidation

'I have a dream...'
What is your dream, your goal?

Looking at each Sephira, how has it been reflected in your life?

- ❖ Tiphareth: Balance

- ❖ Geburah: What needs cutting away

- ❖ Chesed: Opportunities

Astrology
Look at the Sun, Mars and Jupiter in your chart. What information do they give you?

Tarot cards

Put the following cards on a table in their relevant positions:

- ❖ Lust/Strength horizontally

- ❖ Adjustment/Justice at a 45-degree angle on the left

- ❖ The Hermit at a 45-degree angle on the right

The route the cards are taking

Look at the cards, analyse them and think about how they might work with the Sephiroth and in your life.

Lust runs between Geburah and Chesed. It asks you to take hold of the beast, to take control and to ride your dream all the way to manifestation.

What does this tell you about your soul? What goes, what stays, what balancing act are you performing?

Remember that even as you work on that soul level, everything must be earthed. How is the energy coming back to Earth?

'I have learned...'

Ask questions, let your intuition flow. Think, *Planets*, *Sephiroth*, *cards*, *images*, *meditations*, *experiences*, and put it all together to come up with a statement that begins:

From the soul triangle I have learned...

To help you finish this section, here's a meditation you can do when you've finished your consolidation.

Exercise: Vision of the soul triangle

Prepare in the usual way.

Sit down, relax and close your eyes. Begin to breathe 4-2-4-2.

❖ Allow the material world to melt away and make your way to the forest, the clearing and into the Tree.

❖ Sandalphon is waiting for you. He guides you to the pillars. Stand in front of them, ebony on your left, ivory on your right.

❖ As you face the pillars, you see that a curtain, a thin veil, is hanging across the centre of them.

❖ Sandalphon asks you to look through the veil.

❖ As you look, the violet light of Yesod gives way to the green of Netzach and then the golden yellow of Tiphareth.

❖ As the light clears, you see rolling green hills and on one of the hills a cross. In the distance is a white marble cathedral of simple lines bathed in what seems to be a rainbow.

❖ Archangel Michael stands before it, splendid in his coat of many colours, reminding you that it takes different energies to form a whole being.

❖ The image fades and you begin to see a ruby red light.

❖ As it melts away, you see a castle keep. It has iron gates and windows and red walls, walls that seem to be hewn from rubies.

❖ Through a window, you glimpse a room with a black and white floor. A chair is in the centre of it, with 42 others surrounding it in a horseshoe shape.

❖ Khamael stands there, fierce and ready for battle, reminding you that sometimes you must stand your ground.

❖ As his image fades, you see the sapphire blue of Chesed appear and you hear a wind whistling around you.

❖ As the blue light fades, you see a mountain top with a sapphire blue building at its peak.

❖ Climbing that mountain is a line of pilgrims, making their way in devotion to the temple. More pilgrims are going down, smiling at the success of their venture.

❖ In the garden you may see many Masters. Do you recognize any?

❖ You will also see Tzadkiel, resplendent in his robes. He appears as an old man, wise and ready to share his wisdom.

❖ When you're ready, let that image fade and bring yourself back to Malkuth.

❖ Sandalphon will guide you back to the altar.

❖ Thank him.

❖ Make your way out of the temple and into the clearing, then into the forest.

❖ Now bring yourself back to your usual surroundings.

Get out your journal. Write down what you saw, felt, thought and want to get started on right away! Remember to eat and drink something, as this is symbolic of grounding your energy here on Earth.

Next you're going to look at the final triangle, of course the one primarily concerned with your spiritual self, but first a stopover at the Sephira that isn't a Sephira!

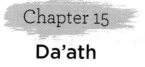

Chapter 15

Da'ath

Here we meet a point on the Tree that isn't a Sephira. Halfway between Tiphareth and Kether, it sits on the Middle Pillar and its keyword is 'Knowledge', but it's knowledge without understanding or wisdom and is sometimes called the Abyss.

It reminds me of those who have studied and know amazing things, but have never used that knowledge, fully felt it or had the opportunity to show their wisdom, or indeed sought that opportunity.

On your journeys on the Tree of Life you won't go into Da'ath, you will go over or around it, and that can give it a certain mystique. That does of course mean people are attracted to it. Often students will see the keywords of the Tree and go straight for 'Knowledge', ignoring everything else and barely stopping to see this circle is not of the Tree and is usually denoted by a dotted line to remind us all of that.

But the knowledge of Da'ath is very important, and if it's used rather than worn like a badge, it guides you towards understanding and on up the Tree.

Some people get lost here, confusing the knowledge they gain with some sort of divinity or enlightenment when in fact all they have is knowledge of what that should be or look like – which is nothing like feeling, seeing and being it.

Some consider Da'ath to be a melting pot of mistakes, of things that really didn't go to the divine plan and are waiting to be recycled in some way, shape or form. That may very well be the case when you consider that's how we move from knowledge to understanding – through our mistakes.

When I teach Qabalah, Da'ath Vader has to be mentioned, the dark lord with all that knowledge, the black cloak and the voice, that unmistakable voice! *Vader* means 'father' and the voice synchronizes too, as this is the point on the Tree of Life that sits across your throat. Art imitating the Tree of Life? Hardly. The Tree of Life influencing art, as it has for centuries.

Da'ath is also linked to the doorway of the Qlippoth, to what is sometimes called the Tree of Death, the reverse image of the Tree of Life. This is sometimes seen as some sort of evil twin, but the reality is the Qlippoth are more akin to the vices of the Sephiroth, and therefore part of a choice we all make. You can use Geburah to do the right thing or you can use it to go on some sort of rampage, Tiphareth to help others or to help yourself, and so on.

Some see the Abyss then as that file on your computer, the one where your half-baked failures are put, but, as previously stated, you have learned from them. You just don't want to dwell on them too much. But hey, here if you need me!

Astrology

The planetary association for Da'ath is one that's open to debate. Some place Uranus here, some Neptune, but Pluto seems to fit more for me. Pluto, Lord of the Underworld, describes the depths of Da'ath, where powerful truths can be found by those adept enough to hear them as knowledge and ready to turn that knowledge from being into doing.

Leaping the Abyss

We live in a world that often feeds our fears. What Da'ath offers you is a way to make sense of all that nonsense. It shows you that worry, fantasy and concerns about what might happen next week or in the next hundred years are just holding you on some higher level of inertia that will no doubt be expressed in your daily life with the words 'What's the point?' As you'll see, the point is in Kether, literally. So Da'ath wakes you up, calls rubbish on it all and shovels it out the back door.

Take that leap of faith and believe not just in yourself but in the support of those divine powers waiting for you above and supporting you from below.

In order to take the leap across the Abyss, you must be sure you're working from your most divine nature rather than being caught in false enlightenment. So, are you working for the good of others or the good of yourself?

Correspondences

The correspondences of Da'ath are tricky, as the symbolism of Da'ath is the absence of symbolism! But here are some of those commonly quoted:

- *Keyword:* Knowledge

- *Archangel:* Mesukiel, Veiler of God

- *Order of angels:* Serpents

- *Planet:* Pluto

- *Virtue:* Self-knowledge

- *Vice:* Self-delusion, false enlightenment

- *Crystals:* Moldavite, obsidian

- *Body part:* Throat

- *Tarot cards:* All cards

Exercise: Leaping over Da'ath

There is no temple working in Da'ath, but take some time to contemplate what irrational fears may be holding you back, where a leap of faith is needed or if you're using the knowledge you have to better your time on Earth and that of others.

By now you may also be feeling as if things that once mattered to you don't matter anymore, especially when you look at the true cost of technology and fashion, for example? Not that I'm advocating wearing robes and telling the time by the rising of the Sun, though that does sound heavenly to me!

Whatever your opinion on that one, you will have noticed many changes in your life by now, and as you move into the realms of the spirit there will be many more. Here you see the immense and true being you are.

Chapter 16

Binah

Binah is called the Great Mother, the Cosmic Goddess. She is the great sea from where we all spring; she is where life begins and ends. She turns both knowledge and wisdom into understanding. Knowledge is something we constantly seek, wisdom is sharing what we have learned, and the alchemy of putting them both together, as Binah does, truly produces a deeper understanding of what we are about.

This is where you have been through some tough stuff, you know what the lesson was and you can see the wisdom that's pointed out to you by your friends, or appears in your dreams, or any other way you can imagine, and then, then there's that moment of deep understanding, that slow stealth of the 'Aha!' moment that almost makes you laugh (sometimes actually does for me) at the deep, deep truth in what you now know to be absolute.

It may seem odd having Binah, the Great Mother, at the head of the Pillar of Severity, and indeed she's represented by Saturn, a male planet and god. But remember that as you climb the Tree you are moving further and further away from the physical world, so when talk turns to male and female, it's not the same as here on Earth, where we divide those forces according to anatomy. Here it's about polarity and a recognition that for black to be, white must exist, for yin there must be yang, for negative, positive, and so on. But if you stop and think for a moment, your own anatomy doesn't determine your response to a situation – you can be both receptive as well as active, negative as well as positive. Both/and rather than either/or.

On the Tree of Life, Binah is seen as a feminine force, one that takes the seed of an idea from Chokmah, binds it with her power into form and sends it down the Tree. Saturn also represents karma, and as Binah sits above Geburah, this planetary force reminds us also of what we have learned, enforcing the discipline of the law of karma – every action has an equal or opposite reaction.

Binah makes all things holy, as she effectively brings all things into formation! She has three names, known as the sanctifying intelligence of the Tree of Life:

- First is Marah, the great sea, and that refers to the cosmic sea, the sea of life.

- Second is Aimah, the fertile mother, and the force that rises from the sea just as humanity did from the Earth's seas.

- Finally there is Ama, the dark mother. There are goddesses up and down the Tree, but in Binah we see Hecate, Persephone, Nuit and many other dark mothers capable of harnessing the power of the universe!

Binah witnesses your sorrow, she sees it and she feels it, but she doesn't seek to make things better, to wrap you in the protectiveness of Chesed or stand in front of you with the might of Geburah. She neither judges nor advises; she accepts and she loves.

There is sorrow in every life, and for me, the beauty in the understanding of Binah is seen in those moments of grief. That may seem like a very odd thing to say. But if you can sit with your grief, feel it and not try to do anything but be with it, there's a beauty in giving in to it, being at one with it, which will heal you more quickly than trying to push it away and pretend it's not there.

Whilst running workshops, past-life and Qabalah workshops in particular, I find there can often be a moment when someone makes a breakthrough, a moment when bottled-up grief comes to the surface and comes out. As tempting as it is to offer comfort, a shoulder to lean on, to be Chesed or even Geburah, if it's a mate of yours who has been hurt, consider the power of Binah, of allowing someone to feel that grief, to finally and totally understand where it comes from and to release it. Silence. The virtue of Binah.

Binah is a tough taskmaster. This Sephira understands when her children need to fly the nest and will push them out, knowing they will be fine but must find their own way, safe in the knowledge that she will be there should they need support and, of course, ready to remind them of the rules. But she will also stand by the sea, weeping as she watches her children leave.

Angels

Tzaphkiel is the archangel of Binah. He protects you from strife and should be called upon whenever you feel things are little too full on, perhaps when you are in need of some support in dealing with what seems like a massive change. He will bring clarity to the situation, showing you what's really going on, what the changes are about and how you can learn from them and work with them, rather than let them take over. He can ease the work of Saturn if you call on him. Change will happen, but perhaps you don't need it to be so tough? He's also said to be so vast that you never see all of him, perhaps just an eye or a hand.

The angelic order is the Aralim, the mighty ones, angels of understanding, known as angels of divine justice.

Vices and virtues

The vice of Binah is avarice, where greed gets in the way of what's needed perhaps.

The virtue is silence. When you listen, you understand, and when you say nothing, you see more. Nothing works better than a silent response – it encourages those who talk too much to carry on talking until they eventually speak their truth rather than what they think you want to hear. At its most effective, it leaves someone with rather too much to say with nowhere to go with their argument and leaves the power with you. Perhaps the modern equivalent is the internet troll. Throw nothing their way and they shrivel!

Tarot cards

The threes of the Tarot are strong structures – a triangle is stronger than a square – but show that hard work is required and (of course) structure needs to be put around your goal.

- *Three of Wands:* Lord of Virtue. Become more aware of the skills and talents you possess.

- *Three of Cups:* Lord of Abundance. The universal love for you is overflowing, exhilarating.

- *Three of Swords:* Lord of Sorrow. Pain and separation. Perhaps something that needs to be tackled when you feel stronger?

- *Three of Disks:* Lord of Works. Find what needs your attention and put your attention on it until it budges!

Exercise: Silence is golden

One of the things I particularly like about Binah is its silence. In saying nothing you can say so much. Binah is a quiet place, which may be why understanding comes to you there. Stopping amidst a storm will show you just where the storm came from and what must happen for calmer seas to take its place.

So this exercise is deceptively simple – but very effective. It may seem like something and nothing, but I know many students who find it a tough thing to do.

It's simply being silent.

If you could do it for half a day, that would be great – in fact it would be amazing. Some people can't do it for 10 minutes.

The purpose of the silence is to allow your inner chatter to wear itself out, to stop banging on about phone contracts and cat litter, to let the noise of your inner personality die down and to begin to listen with more clarity to your soul and spirit.

You don't have to sit cross-legged meditating – in fact it's best if you don't. You should just be. Wander by the ocean if you can, as the sound of the waves and the motion of the ocean will help you empty your mind. No plugging in your MP3 player and listening to some tunes. Remember the exercise is done in silence. Complete silence isn't easy in a noisy world, but if it's just you and nature, that's perfect.

When you find that place where the noise dies down and you reach the heaven of no internal noise, no external distractions, I promise you, you'll feel more connected to the universe and from it will come a greater understanding of yourself, what happens next and what choices need to be made. You are Binah, you are the Great Mother, you can let go and leave it to fate.

When you feel you've done enough, write down your experience. Was that tougher than you thought? What information came from your soul? Do you recognize just how much your personality witters on all the time?

Then make it a habit: a few hours or a half a day a week where silence is indeed golden.

Visiting Binah

Correspondences

- *Keyword:* Understanding

- *Number:* Three

- *Archangel:* Tzaphkiel

- *Order of angels:* Aralim

- *Planet:* Saturn

- *Virtue:* Silence

- *Vice:* Avarice

- *Gods/goddesses:* Danu, Demeter, Hecate, Hera, Isis, Nuit, Shakti

- *Colour:* Black

- *Crystals:* Jet, onyx, pearl

- *Incense:* Myrrh

- *Body part:* Right side of the face

- *Tarot cards:* The threes, the queens

Exercise: The Temple of Binah

Dress your altar in silence. Pick a time and place that you know will be as still as possible.

Take a Tarot card before your meditation.

Perform your protection and energy work and create your sacred and beautiful space according to your own divine creativity.

Ask your guides, Archangel Tzaphkiel and the divine beings of Binah to assist you.

Use your 4-2-4-2 breathing or any technique you're comfortable with to count yourself down into a meditative state of being.

❖ Allow the material world to melt away and replace it with the temple forest. See it, feel it, be in it completely and walk silently through it.

❖ Once you're in the garden, perhaps already in the clearing, see your Tree. This time it will be a piece of jet that breaks free from the shifting, sombre branches of the Tree of Life.

❖ As it forms a black sphere in front of you, walk towards it, considering what Binah means to you. Where you need to be more like the Great Mother? What needs the discipline of form in your life?

❖ Project the symbol for Saturn onto the sphere as you walk into it and through into the worlds of Binah. Step onto her beach and feel the dark water lap at your toes.

❖ Consider the lessons and gifts of Binah and how you could use them. What's relevant to you right here, right now?

❖ Feel the holiness of this space, home to the Great Mother. It is a very sacred place.

❖ Consider your own inner Goddess and your inner God, the balance of the feminine and masculine principles within you. Feel them work together in perfect symmetry.

❖ Surrender to the silence. In doing so, you find your consciousness expands like never before, right across the great ocean of Binah to the truth of your life in Malkuth. Observe.

❖ The temple of Binah is triangular, made of many triangles in fact, but it is also the beach and the ocean.

❖ The archangel of Binah, Tzaphkiel, comes towards you. You think it's him, for he's difficult to see, easier to feel. He can help lift the burden of grief, but he can't remove it; he can ease your troubles, but can't do the work for you.

❖ Ask him for the vision of sorrow – how you work with the virtue of Binah and avoid the vice.

❖ Commune further with Tzaphkiel and the Great Mother and if they offer you a gift, offer them one in the form of your commitment to pay more attention to when silence is required and to work with the balance of yin and yang more within yourself.

❖ When you're ready, follow the path back from the ocean and towards the dark sphere waiting for you.

❖ Say your farewells, pay any further respects and walk into the black light, back into the temple forest of Malkuth.

❖ Allow the forest to fade, return to your usual surroundings and then close your meditation down.

Make notes, take a Tarot card and remember to eat and drink something. No matter how small, it's symbolic of grounding your energy here on Earth.

Binah consolidation

'Everything has its wonders, even darkness and silence, and I learn, whatever state I may be in, therein to be content.'

HELEN KELLER

'I have a dream...'
Remind yourself of the dream you stated in Malkuth.

Astrology
Look at the planet Saturn in your chart, where he sits and what aspects he attracts. What have you decided to bring more form to and where do you think you need to keep your own counsel a little more?

Tarot cards
❖ Going into the temple: Card

❖ Coming out of the temple: Card

❖ Consolidating the temple: Card

The route the cards are taking
A short analysis of what the cards tell you.

Analysis of the temple visualization
How you felt, what you saw, what the symbols mean to you.

How it has manifested in your life
How has it presented itself in your life here on Earth? What have you noticed that you missed before? What do you want to change?

'Moving forward, I commit to...'
Make a commitment to making those changes happen.

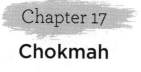

Chapter 17

Chokmah

Sitting opposite Binah is the divine force of Chokmah, the supernal Father, the divine masculine. In unison with Binah and Kether above this triangle, this trilogy, is in effect the Creator in whatever way you want to perceive God, Goddess, Source. Let there be light!

This high on the Tree, it becomes difficult to put it all into words. Even in the beautiful realms of unbounded meditation, it's hard to understand. So don't try. Just feel, sense, let the energy move around and through you and be in these worlds.

In Chokmah energy is key. This is the life-force itself. Given form in Binah, it's that spark that ignites the power of Kether, the emanation and source that illuminates every Sephira on the Tree of Life. Ignited by Chokmah, you see it in your aura, you see it in the trees and feel it through the Earth, you are it and it is you. You receive it and transmit to it, join with it and feel it buzzing through every fibre of your being when you're still enough to listen. It's what you wish would come out of your fingers when you play witches and wizards, and the truth is it does.

The cattle prod of the Tree, it zaps things into action, into being, and asks you to make that choice: what plans need an extra push? What creative ideas, applied with logic, could give birth to a new way of doing things? What could take your plans in a more beneficial direction? Whatever the answer, Chokmah throws the switch to 'on'.

The keyword given to Chokmah is 'Wisdom'. A word to the wise – it's not the same as knowledge. The modern saying explains this so well: 'Knowledge is knowing a tomato is a fruit; wisdom is knowing it won't go well in a fruit salad.' Wisdom that hasn't been expressed is understanding and knowledge – both fine things, but until they are applied, made manifest in some way, they are but that. Nice that you know that, great that you understand, but let's hear your wisdom. Having hidden away for years sometimes, it's clear to me just how important this is. None of us should hold our knowledge and understanding to our own souls when the wisdom of sharing it could make a difference, no matter how small or how grand.

Few of us are wise all of the time: if only. It's also something that takes lifetimes to learn. The soul grows into it and the use of the power of Chokmah shines from some and is sadly lacking in others. But knowing and understanding where it sits on the Tree of Life can put you closer to finding that wisdom in yourself when you need it most.

Angels

Ratziel is the archangel of Chokmah. He guides the creative force and is the keeper of mysteries. *The Book of Ratziel* is the book of stars. The symbol for Uranus and therefore

Chokmah, looks like a television aerial and this perfectly describes how Ratziel transmits to those who stop to listen in meditation: he transmits the consciousness of all the ancient, wise dimensions in the inner and outer universe to us here on Earth.

The order of angels is the Auphamim, the wheels, whirling forces of creation with many eyes. The wheel, moving things along – the wheel of the seasons and the zodiac perhaps?

Astrology

Uranus is assigned to Chokmah and finding him in your natal chart will bring your personal information about this energy. This planet can be disruptive but, like its Qabalistic counterpart, it can bring logical solutions that seem to come out of the blue. Wherever you find Uranus in your chart, you're likely to find a part of your life that always seems to be in state of flux, but also a part of your life where you're at your most creative.

The zodiac wheel itself is a symbol for Chokmah, an ever-changing theatre of inspiration, planetary movement and possibilities waiting to be uncovered, and hopefully you've realized that by now. Your consolidations will have shown you that.

Don't underestimate the value of the zodiac, of astrology. The guiding principle of 'as above, so below' is a powerful one. Astrology has been and will continue to be challenged and belittled, but so will anything that has the ability to remind you of your amazing place in the universe and how unique and empowered you are.

Vices and virtues

There is no vice in Chokmah. The virtue is devotion – devotion to the divine life-force expressed in the Tree.

Tarot cards

The four twos are the Tarot cards associated with Chokmah. They represent the balance brought about by two energies working together rather than one trying to do it all on its own. The twos remind you that in order to feel whole, the ying and the yang should be present – polarity in its purest form.

- *Two of Wands:* Lord of Dominion. Make your choices. Be true to your own sovereignty to have the life you want.

- *Two of Cups:* Lord of Love. Self-love expressed through harmonious polarization.

- *Two of Swords:* Lord of Peace. The mind is at peace, taking the higher ground from a place of wisdom.

- *Two of Disks:* Lord of Change. Things change, and so they should, as inertia is prevented by constant change. What needs to be changed?

Words to be wise

Ten little prompts:

1. Wisdom isn't about age, it's about experience, so plan a trip, travel, listen to the wise folks around you and listen with more than your ears.

2. A wise person has a deeper understanding of life's experiences. Don't get caught up in the small stuff.

3. So now that you're not sweating the small stuff, you can see what lessons the small stuff taught you. Life has educated you.

4. Now share some of the stuff you do have.

5. Meditate. Find what works for you and be regular with your practice. Find your balancing-point.

6. Growing up doesn't mean growing old. Climb a tree now and again.

7. Challenge the status quo. Use the experience of Chokmah to re-invent anything you see that needs to have that wisdom applied to it. Write it down.

8. Don't compare, ever. You're a unique spark from the Tree of Life. Shine like you know it. Make it a foundation of your life.

9. Look down the Tree and see what you have learned. Remember the road to true wisdom is to 'Know thyself' here on Earth.

10. Take all the above and apply it to helping others.

Visiting Chokmah

Correspondences

- Keyword: Wisdom

- Number: Two

- Archangel: Ratziel

- Order of angels: Auphamim

- Planet: Uranus

- Virtue: Devotion

- Vice: None

- Gods/goddesses: Odin, Osiris, Pan, Shiva, Thoth, Uranus, Zeus

- Colour: Grey

- Crystals: Jade, tourmaline, turquoise

- Incense: Musk

- Body part: Left side of the face

- Tarot cards: The twos

Exercise: The Temple of Chokmah

Dress your altar to look like a night full of shining stars and the light of the universe with all its promises yet to be manifested.

Take a Tarot card before your meditation.

Perform your protection and energy work. Create your sacred and beautiful space according to your own divine creativity.

Ask your guides, Archangel Ratziel and the divine beings of Chokmah to assist you.

Use your 4-2-4-2 breathing or any technique you're comfortable with to count yourself down into a meditative state of being.

❖ Allow the material world to melt away and replace it with the temple forest. See it, feel it, be in it completely.

❖ Once you're in the garden, perhaps already in the clearing, see your Tree. This time it will be a piece of turquoise that breaks free from the shifting, sparkling branches of the Tree of Life.

❖ As it forms a sphere in front of you, walk towards it, considering what Chokmah means to you. Where does the Great Father manifest in your life?

❖ Project the symbol for Uranus onto the sphere, which has now turned grey, and you walk into it and through into the starry worlds of Chokmah.

❖ There is no temple. Chokmah appears as a straight line, a hallway to the stars and beyond.

❖ Consider the lessons and gifts of Chokmah and how you could use them. What's relevant to you right here, right now?

❖ Walk along the path and commune with any beings of Chokmah that come your way and the Great Father all around you.

❖ You may catch a glimpse of the great zodiac wheel of life spinning in space. Which sign shines the brightest? What does it illuminate in your own chart?

❖ The archangel of Chokmah is Ratziel and you feel his presence rather than see him. What impressions do you have? Does he share any secrets from his great book of mysteries?

❖ Ask him for a vision of the Source, how it looks to you on your path right now, how it shows itself in your life and how you can use it.

❖ Commune further with Ratziel or any beings of Chokmah, and as they offer you a gift, offer them one in return in the form of how you intend to use this great vision.

❖ When you're ready, follow the path back down the hallway and towards your grey sphere.

- ❖ Say your farewells, pay any further respects and walk into the grey light and back into the temple forest of Malkuth.

- ❖ Allow the forest to fade, return to your usual surroundings and close down your meditation.

Take a Tarot card, make notes and remember to eat and drink something. No matter how small, it's symbolic of grounding your energy here on Earth.

Chokmah consolidation

'The work of the individual still remains the spark that moves mankind ahead even more than teamwork.'

IGOR SIKORSKY, AVIATOR

'I have a dream...'
Remind yourself of the dream you stated in Malkuth.

Astrology
Look at the planet Uranus. Where do you use your ability to bring about change, sometimes sudden? Where does your wisdom sit? What is the source of your own power?

Tarot cards
- ❖ Going into the temple: Card

- ❖ Coming out of the temple: Card

- ❖ Consolidating the temple: Card

The route the cards are taking
A short analysis of what the cards tell you.

Analysis of the temple visualization
How you felt, what you saw, what the symbols mean to you.

How it has manifested in your life
How has it presented itself in your life here on Earth? What have you noticed that you missed before? What do you want to change?

'Moving forward, I commit to...'
Make a commitment to making those changes happen.

Chapter 18

Kether

This is the crown, sitting at the top of the Tree, over your crown chakra on your physical body (above the head, not on it). Until this point you know nothing, no-thing, but here you just might know something is going on – not much, but something. Governed by Neptune and sitting at the very top of this magical tree, it's not the easiest of places to understand, but isn't that the point? Would you expect anything less from the end and beginning of your mystical journey? In this state of being there's no action, no reaction, and it's supposed to be that vague. Attempting to over-analyse it will make you feel dizzy, if you're not already.

Imagine Kether at the top of your Tree, the highest viewpoint, but whilst standing in Kether looking down, it would be just as easy to imagine standing at the base of a Tree looking up. Kether is the root if you count down numerically – it's number one, Chokmah is number two, Binah number three, and so on. It's rooted in the heavens – perhaps we are the ones waving about in the wind? This wonderful symbol reminds us that 'as above, so below', that all that comes to us below is from above, from our true root.

But you aren't standing at the top, you're currently living in the world of Assiah, the world of the physical, and as such, looking up in wonder, you can never fully immerse yourself in the world of Kether. Never fully immerse yourself and still return to a physical body, that is. So it appears veiled, protecting you from the blinding light. God looks down. Humanity looks up.

I've found that the more you talk about Kether, the further away your understanding of it goes. Your words chase away the gentle clouds of the divine nature of all there is.

To enter Kether, as much as you can (and that's really not a lot), you don't have to *do* anything, but you do have to *be* everything, and all at once! Impossible? You're doing it right now; what's impossible is naming it, putting into words, describing the feeling or the knowing, and that's perhaps why from the Source it falls down through the Sephiroth like water through a filtration system, with each sphere taking out its special power to help you identify at least some of it. But you're a human being, not a human's doing. So perhaps Kether isn't as far away as you might think.

The God name for Kether is Ehyeh, 'I Am' or 'I Am That I Am'. No titles: I Am. And so, too, are you. You are your own Kether, I Am That I Am, ready to move into action via Chokmah's wisdom and Binah's understanding down the Tree of Life.

Imagine the power when you not only recognize that energy, but also feel it within you – creative and all-encompassing spiritual energy holding the divine plan that, once activated, will come down your Tree into the Sephiroth of the soul and manifest via the Sephiroth of the personality. What force, what form, what magic will you bring from your very own Kether?

Astrology

There's much debate about planetary rulership for Kether. Some will say Uranus, others Pluto, but for me, Neptune is the only planet that brings the qualities of Kether alive. Neptune's nature is to lose himself in order to find what he is looking for and to suddenly come out with the answer. This is also the planet of the mystic, the seeker of magical knowledge, and with Uranus as Chokmah beside him, Kether must be about as magical as it gets.

Angels

The archangel is Metatron. For me, he always appears as a small child, but for others he is enormous. He is said to be the closest to the Source, God. Whatever you choose to call the divine, Metatron is his/her right-hand man, the prince of archangels. His help is often needed when struggling with concepts that are just beyond the veil. You know something is solvable, but you just can't get through that candyfloss, marshmallow moment ... enter Metatron.

As mentioned earlier, Metatron was once Enoch on the Earth plane, while his brother Sandalphon was Elijah. Two great beings who were once human are at the top and base of the Tree of Life.

The angelic order is the Chioyh ha Qodesh, the holy living creatures. They can live in the pure holiness of this Sephira and appear as burning coals of fire. They are to Kether what the Cherubim are to Malkuth – those who set the pattern and make it work.

Vices and virtues

There is no vice. The virtue of Kether is attainment, the completion of the Great Work.

Tarot cards

The four aces really don't need much of an introduction. They are the first rush of energy of their suits, Fire, Earth, Air and Water, reminding you that in Kether the elements of Malkuth are far from forgotten.

- *Ace of Wands:* The beginning of a new life – a new creative project or literally a new life, a baby.

- *Ace of Cups:* The beginning of a new relationship, the granting of a wish or perhaps the inspiration to begin something new.

- *Ace of Swords:* Clarity. Obstacles are removed and you can see your way through.

- *Ace of Disks:* A new job, the start of a new project or perhaps becoming more involved with Earth conservation.

Exercise: Building the Tree on your body

It seems only fitting to do a meditation at this point, one that will remind you how far you've come and will go some way to building the Tree of Life on you and reminding of where it sits physically. You have been doing this on the astral plane since day one.

Do your Qabalistic Cross (*see page 66*).

Prepare in the usual way.

Sit down, relax and close your eyes. Begin to breathe 4-2-4-2.

❖ See before you a glowing Tree of Life.

❖ Look at the Sephiroth. See them glowing, colourful and vibrating with energy.

❖ Now turn your back on the Tree. Put your spine on the Middle Pillar.

❖ First, make sure your feet are firmly rooted in Malkuth. See them anchored in the Earth, your home for now.

❖ Now focus your attention on your groin area. See Yesod glowing violet and silver.

❖ Next see Hod, orange and sitting on your right hip.

❖ Move when you're ready to the emerald sphere of Netzach, on your left hip.

❖ Now on to the yellow sphere of Tiphareth over your solar plexus and heart.

❖ Next see the ruby red of Geburah on your right arm.

❖ And the sapphire blue of Chesed on your left.

❖ To the right of your head, see and feel the black Sephira of Binah.

❖ To your left, the grey circle of Chokmah.

- ❖ Now, above your head, see Kether.

- ❖ Sit with this image.

- ❖ Do any of the Sephiroth appear dull, maybe in need of some extra energy?

- ❖ If any do, send them that extra energy, but use the lightning flash to balance them all – remember, no Sephira works on its own. Start with Kether, move to Chokmah, onto Binah and towards Chesed, across to Geburah and over to Tiphareth, through to Netzach and back to Hod, towards Yesod, back into Malkuth and down through your feet into the Earth, where you can secure and ground your energy.

- ❖ When you're ready, bring your awareness back into the room and wiggle your fingers and toes.

Write down your experience. If you get any further inspiration, jot it down!

Visiting Kether

Correspondences

- Keyword: Crown

- Number: One

- Archangel: Metatron

- Order of angels: Chioyh ha Qodesh

- Planet: Neptune

- Virtue: Attainment, completion of the Great Work

- Vice: None

- Gods/goddesses: Zeus, Jupiter, Ptah, Ra, Modron, Parabraham

- Colour: White brilliance

- Crystal: Diamond

- Incense: Ambergris

- Body part: Cranium

- Tarot cards: The four aces

Exercise: The light of Kether

Remember this path is an experience. You don't touch Kether in its highest form – you can't whilst you're in physical form, but you can go some way to understanding it as it's reflected down the Tree.

As you prepare your altar, think *White, white on white…*

Perform your protection and energy work. Create your sacred and beautiful space according to your own divine creativity.

Ask your guides, Archangel Metatron and the divine beings of Kether to assist you.

Use your 4-2-4-2 breathing or any technique you're comfortable with to count yourself down into a meditative state of being.

❖ Allow the material world to melt away and replace it with the temple forest. See it, feel it, be in it completely, but know that it may not be as tangible as usual.

❖ Once you're in the garden, see your Tree. This time it will be a diamond that breaks free from the rainbow-lit, sparkling branches of the Tree of Life.

✦ As it forms a blinding white sphere in front of you, walk towards it, considering what Kether means to you. What do you consider to be the 'Source'?

✦ Project the symbol for Neptune onto the sphere as you walk into it and through into the blinding whiteness of Kether, where you become that light. There is no distinction between you and it; never was, never will be.

✦ The light, you notice, is made of rainbow colours and now and again you catch a glimpse of the refracted light. There is no temple, no structure, only the rainbow light dancing around you.

✦ Metatron, the archangel of Kether, comes towards you, or rather you feel his presence.

✦ Ask him for a vision of the reunion with Source, a vision that's appropriate for you at this stage of your journey.

✦ Commune further with Metatron and the energy of Kether. They will not offer a gift, as visiting Kether is the gift.

✦ When you're ready, follow the path back through to your diamond sphere.

✦ Say your farewells, pay any further respects and walk into the diamond light and back into the temple forest of Malkuth, realizing that Kether is in Malkuth, as Malkuth is in Kether. As above, so below.

✦ Allow the forest to fade. Return to your usual surroundings.

When you have closed down your meditation, take a Tarot card, make notes and remember to eat and drink something. No matter how small, it's symbolic of grounding your energy here on Earth.

Kether consolidation

'A tree you pass by every day is just a tree. If you were to closely examine what a tree has and the life a tree has, even the smallest thing can withstand a curiosity, and you can examine whole worlds.'
WILLIAM SHATNER

'I have a dream...'
Remind yourself of the dream you stated in Malkuth.

Astrology
Find Neptune in your chart. Ask where you dream and lose yourself most. If put to good use, what divine things could come from it?

Tarot cards
❖ Going into the temple: Card

❖ Coming out of the temple: Card

❖ Consolidating the temple: Card

The route the cards are taking
A short analysis of what the cards tell you.

Analysis of the temple visualization
How you felt, what you saw, what the symbols mean to you.

How it has manifested in your life
How has it presented itself in your life here on Earth? What have you noticed that you missed before? What do you want to change?

'Moving forward, I commit to...'
Make a commitment to making those changes happen.

The spiritual triangle consolidation

So here we are, the last triangle, and of course it's the spiritual one. It's not easy to grasp some of these concepts and put shapes and forms around them, but that's what Qabalah offers, a way of putting even the most abstract ideas into action and refining them until they become tangible and workable.

'I have a dream...'

What is your dream, your goal?

Looking at each Sephira, how has it been reflected in your life?

- ❖ Binah: Form
- ❖ Chokmah: Flash of inspiration
- ❖ Netzach: Wear your crown!

Astrology

Look at Saturn, Uranus and Neptune in your chart. What information do they give you?

Tarot cards

Put the following cards on a table in their relevant positions:

- ❖ The Empress horizontally
- ❖ The Magician/Magus at a 45-degree angle on the left
- ❖ The Fool at a 45-degree angle on the right

The route the cards are taking

Look at the cards, analyse them and think about how they might work with the Sephiroth and in your life.

What does this tell you about your spiritual approach to life? What form does it take? Do you feel you pause now, make wiser choices?

'I have learned...'

Ask questions, let your intuition flow. Think, *Planets, Sephiroth, cards, images, meditations, experiences*, and put it all together to come up with a statement that begins:

From the spiritual triangle I have learned...

Now it's time for a meditation.

Exercise: Vision of the spiritual triangle

Prepare in the usual way.

Sit down, relax and close your eyes. Begin to breathe 4-2-4-2.

❖ Allow the material world to melt away and make your way to the forest, the clearing and into the Tree.

❖ Sandalphon is waiting for you. He guides you to the pillars. Stand in front of them, ebony on your left, ivory on your right.

❖ As you face the pillars, you see that a curtain, a thin veil, is hanging across the centre of them.

❖ Sandalphon asks you to look through the veil.

❖ The violet light of Yesod will give way to the green of Netzach and fading in now will be the golden yellow light of Tiphareth

❖ As that wanes, the ruby red of Geburah appears and as it fades the sapphire blue of Chesed appears.

❖ Then you hear the ocean and see a woman on a cliff edge, looking out to sea, waiting for a loved one to return.

❖ Can you glimpse Tzaphkiel? Perhaps the dark shadow of his armour?

- As the vision of Binah fades, you see space, outer space, a starlit sky, and from nowhere comes a spinning zodiac wheel. Which sign lights up for you? It may not be your own Sun sign.

- Ratziel stands on the wheel, in the sign of Aquarius. He sparks with electricity, energy constantly in movement.

- That image will now fade and you will be left with a white veil. And just when you think the show is over you catch a glimpse of ... what was that?

- There it is again. Maybe it's your imagination? You can't explain it, you can't touch it. Nothing's there – or is it?

- Perhaps it's Metatron, waiting for you to be crowned as the ruler of your own kingdom.

- When you're ready, let that image fade and bring yourself back to Malkuth.

- Sandalphon leads you back from the pillars. Thank him for your time here.

- Make your way out of the temple, into the clearing, then into the forest.

- Now bring yourself back to your usual surroundings.

Take a Tarot card, make notes and remember to eat and drink something.

And now it's time for one final exercise...

Exercise: This is me!

Who you truly are, the shining being you truly are. One page. Go! Don't hold back. What have you discovered about yourself on your journey up the Tree?

Part III

THE 22 PATHS

Chapter 19

Working with the Paths

The hardest part of writing this book hasn't been what to put in, it's been what to leave out. This is a book about the basics of Qabalah and my intention in writing it has been to spark your interest, to encourage you to look more closely at what Qabalah has to offer. If you would like to do that, perhaps find a local group or maybe an online course you feel safe and happy with and then make it yours and work with it the way you want to do it.

By now you will have seen the system, the way that it works, and the intellectual side of you will be getting to grips with the words and concepts. It will then enter your life and you'll see it physically, and then there's the magical part, where meditation illuminates the details and you form bonds with the esoteric worlds that begin to walk alongside you, helping, encouraging. Your world changes. Your worlds change.

The paths work the same way, but they do require some strong boots and the appropriate clothing. I am including them as a reference only. They will help you understand the major arcana of the Tarot more – help you to see where that fits into the structure of the Tree of Life – but there will be no pathworking meditations or experiences, as those may be a little more than basic.

Leaving the paths out is leaving a very large part of the map out. They all have their own symbols and correspondences, just like the Sephiroth, for they are all part of the Tree. When you're ready, and under further instruction, they will provide you with some incredible experiences. But I must reiterate, they must be trodden with expert guidance and at a level suitable to your knowledge. This is but a tiny, tiny, peek.

The paths

So, let's begin back at the bottom, with the path from Malkuth to Yesod. But remember these paths can trodden from Kether to Malkuth, too.

Path 32: The Universe

Malkuth to Yesod

The world, the universe – it's where you incarnate and where you rise through the planes. The first and last path is an ascent into the realms of your higher self, but also of descent into your subconscious and all that it holds. Remember your subconscious forgets nothing. No-thing. This is Malkuth to Yesod, that shift in your perception as you see the great machinery of the universe and the magic that really makes the world go round. It is completion, but also the beginning. Here Persephone moves into the underworld to join her lover, Hades, and leaves her mother, Demeter, weeping by the lake. But she will be back, born again.

Path 31: Judgement/The Aeon

Malkuth to Hod

Who? Why? When? All these questions and just who is going to provide the answers? The fire in your belly, the desire to learn and find things out, and as this path runs from Malkuth to Hod, it's fitting that the myths are those of fire-bringers like Prometheus, whose curiosity delivered fire to humanity, but at a price. It's about bringing those higher spiritual principles into being rather than leaving them in the realms of the mind. Walking your talk perhaps? And as it links the Akashic Records, in Hod, to Malkuth, it can bring memories of past lives – with the Fire of karmic conditions attached, no doubt!

Path 30: The Sun

Yesod to Hod

The path of enlightenment, Yesod to Hod, connecting the vision of the machinery of the universe to Splendour. As you have seen, the worlds of astral magic and word 'magic' combine, perhaps reminding us of the effectiveness of getting it right above to get it right below?

This path may not flatter you – it may bring all those things you're not so happy about into full view – but it will offer an opportunity to work with them and perhaps to change what you bring back down the Tree. As you move up the path, the gaining of wisdom may not be comfortable, but by the time you are coming down, you will have realized why and will wish to bring that new knowledge to Earth.

Path 29: The Moon

Malkuth to Netzach

From Earthly realms to the world of instincts. So what do *you* think that might be like? When you pause and link into all that you are, you can see your way through, but how often do you pause?

Your primitive nature is inherent within you, it's always there, and this path reminds you of nature and your place within it. This is the path of the Moon, of ebb and flow, of cycles such as the tides, plants and menstruation. In Tarot, The Moon is a divinely feminine card and often signals a need to listen to your inner wisdom, your intuition.

Path 28: The Star

(Sometimes shown as The Emperor and you may use that title if you wish, but this is the path/card I was shown and trained in using.)

Yesod to Netzach

Yesod to Netzach and the sign of Aquarius, the water-bearer, a distinctly feminine card, as you can imagine with Venus and the Moon at its heart. Here you must be aware of glamour and the danger of seeing just the glamour. We would all like our wishes to be fulfilled one day, but pause for a moment to consider the influences here. You already know Yesod is a hall of mirrors and Netzach a world of beauty. As you move up this path, the fay worlds of magic will enchant you, but you must keep your head. Coming down, remember the magic of abundance you can bring into your life.

Path 27: The Tower
Hod to Netzach

Any Tarot reader will tell you the reaction they get when clients see this card. It can often be sharp intake of breath. Why? Because it usually depicts the destruction of a tower, with those building it or inhabiting it being cast to the ground.

Ruled by Mars and running from Hod to Netzach, this path is where we meet the opposing forces of thoughts and feelings. On your Tree of Life you will also see it runs across the point before you make the move into the soul triangle. It's in the personality triangle, the lightning flash runs along it, and if you're not balanced as a personality – able to balance your thoughts and feelings, that is – it will find the weakness, find the blockages and push through. Not always a comfortable experience!

Path 26: The Devil
Hod to Tiphareth

Clearly this is another of those cards people aren't too happy to see. But nothing is as it seems, and that's the lesson of The Devil card. It's about illusion, and illusion may be the result of being ill-informed or choosing to be ignorant of the truth.

Here the goat, a symbol of the card, moves from personality consciousness to soul consciousness. Sometimes this is a dark night of the soul. It was for me.

Wondering what way is up, what is real and what is not? Know your own truths and move slowly, carefully, through the illusions not only of your own personality but also the words of others.

Path 25: Temperance/Art

Yesod to Tiphareth

Standing on the Moon, looking at the Sun, again you don't take this path lightly. Sometimes called the dark night of the soul, it can be one, and it's not one night. This is the moment when your faith is tested, when you must push forward or turn back. The choice is and always will be yours.

As you move up this path, it may feel desolate. You may feel unsupported, and that will be as far from the truth than it's ever been, but you may feel that way. It's your own resources that will see you through, and as you come down the Tree from Tiphareth to Yesod, you will feel your soul shining with love to reflect into this world of Malkuth with all its nonsense.

Path 24: Death

Netzach to Tiphareth

Here's another one of those cards, but as any Tarot reader will tell you, Death is about letting go. It is, in fact, a good thing.

Spiritually speaking, there are seven deaths:

- The first is the union of two forces. No longer self-governing, two become one. Consider that on the Tree for a moment.

- The second death is that of evolution. The rise and fall of nations and species perhaps?

- The third is that of the physical body. Well, that's death and rebirth of course. As you leave one form, you become another; your physical body gives way to release the soul.

- The fourth death is sleep, a release into the astral worlds that's not as severe as number three, you might say.

- The fifth is the death of the personality. When you shake off this mortal coil, you will leave your personality behind and emerge as the soul you are.

- The sixth is trance.

- The seventh is illumination.

So many doing this work walk this path so often, through the work, through their dreams, through the most intense meditations and mini-deaths of the personality where what once seemed so important is no longer so. It's an old friend, Netzach to Tiphareth and the astrological sign of Scorpio.

Path 23: The Hanged Man

Hod to Geburah

Yes, yet another one of those cards and again misunderstood. It shows a man hanging upside down. Encouraging him to look at things from a different perspective perhaps? You would, wouldn't you?!

This is a path that looks at the personality and the soul in unison. It links both triangles, so perhaps, and this is only my opinion, it highlights the comparison between what we think we could do and what we actually do. You may think getting involved in a cause is the right thing to do, but in reality you eat crisps and watch television. Look at things from a different perspective. What can you really do and why aren't you doing it?

Coming back down the Tree, of course that could be karma nagging you to change your mind and change your world.

Path 22: Justice/Adjustment

Tiphareth to Geburah

The scales of justice are waiting for you on this path from Tiphareth to Geburah, waiting to weigh the good and the bad and to see you face the consequences of your actions. The Tarot card shows those scales, and its symbolism reminds you that this moment will come. It comes to all of us.

Path 21: The Wheel of Fortune

Netzach to Chesed

Is it time to set out on a quest? What are you searching for that's intangible but you'll know it when you see it?

The fragrant dreams of Netzach may have you yearning to reach the heights of soul contentment by setting up your retreat somewhere warm where milk (almond milk also available) and honey flow, and if you work with the Tree of Life it's all possible. Yours is an ever-evolving destiny, and when you keep moving and working with The Wheel of Fortune, you'll know when to move forward and when to cling on!

Path 20: The Hermit

Tiphareth to Chesed

How I love this path. What does it mean? Just pause for a moment and consider this: you know what it means, you know what Tiphareth to Chesed means! How great that words you may never have heard of suddenly hold all that power, all those lessons, all those experiences. I love that.

Back to the path. The card shows the Hermit with a lamp, lighting the way, and here the light of Tiphareth lights your way to the mountains of Chesed and the Lords of Peace. The truth is the quest is not done in Chesed, it's a resting place only, but what a resting place!

Path 19: Strength/Lust

Geburah to Chesed

A path that forms not only a major band of energy on the lightning flash but also the top of the soul triangle. Leo the lion shows up in the card, tamed by a young female who has the measure of him, not through brute strength, as you might think, but by the strength of her spirit and how she lives. This is taking your courage and holding it in front of you, for this is the moment when you must have faith and tame your own lion. This is where you show up.

Path 18: The Chariot

Geburah to Binah

The Chariot isn't a quiet mode of transport. It doesn't arrive unannounced, but with a shout. It doesn't hide its light and it shows openly the hard work it's taken to get this far.

Having confidence in who you are, the light you bear and, most importantly, why you bear it and taking full responsibility for it is what this path's all about. Moving from soul to spirit – truly moving from soul to spirit.

When the card is reversed, it's about knowing what destiny you have chosen and accepting your role as the only one who can make it happen.

Path 17: The Lovers

Tiphareth to Binah

Talking of destiny, here's the path from the soul to the spiritual. The Lovers card shows you with your divine holy guardian angel – not another being, but a part of you, the part of you that knows your purpose, your part in the great plan.

Astrologically, it is the sign of Gemini, a sign often accused of having two faces. Not true, but moving on, it's symbolic perhaps of the dual nature of humanity, with the incarnate personality being reflecting the holy guardian angel above. Some people do this very well, others not so, but even if it's not so much, that angel's still there.

Path 16: The Hierophant

Chesed to Chokmah

Parallel to the 18th path, the Chariot path, this path runs from Chesed to Chokmah, and is represented by the astrological sign of Taurus. The card shows a hierophant, a priest and teacher, passing on higher wisdom to two individuals in sacred union. When all of us hold this sacred information, we can properly sit at a round table as equals. This path reminds you to find good teachers, not all Earthly, and to listen to them and work with wisdom in a merciful way, like a good king. Or queen!

Path 15: The Emperor

(For some this is The Star, but, as previously described, I will be using The Emperor, as that is how I was taught!)

Tiphareth to Chokmah

The Emperor is resplendent in his robes and the fiery colours of the card show his association with the sign of Aries and its go-getting energy. The path takes you towards the great wheel of the zodiac and knowing your chart provides your soul with deeper information. Here you take charge of your kingdom with the spark of divine wisdom within you, not only knowing it's there, but knowing how to use it effectively.

Path 14: The Empress

Binah to Chokmah

Another path on the lightning flash linking Binah to Chokmah, the Divine Mother to the Divine Father, at the base of the spiritual triangle. The card usually shows a young woman who is pregnant and it reflects the seed of that first flash of light from Chokmah that takes form in Binah.

Path 13: The High Priestess

Tiphareth to Kether

Across the Abyss, a path walked only when you are ready – and then stop, because you're probably not. Think again, seek again and be truly ready. The way of the Abyss is knowing you are supported. Not hoping, *knowing*.

Path 12: The Magician

Binah to Kether

A path that asks you to see the reality of the world you're living in from a higher spiritual perspective. Mercury and the symbol of the Magician show an ability to bring down this perspective, but look how high up the Tree it is! Of course people are drawn to this image (thank you, Harry Potter), but the truth is that a real magician is years and years in training and sometimes gets it wrong before getting it right.

Path 11: The Fool

Chokmah to Kether

The final path and the first. As you have seen, the higher paths are more abstract, not so easy to put into words, if I am being honest. But I can say that this is a path of endings and beginnings, like the Universe. The Fool has what he needs for the journey ahead (we all do), but it's knowing what to use and when to use it that makes the difference.

So What Now?

What goes up must come down... Now you've visited each Sephira, it's a good idea to do the same but in reverse! This time, however, you're going to look at all of your experiences, your notes in your journal and the astrological and Tarot information and see what it's showing you: how to bring your goal into manifestation (if indeed it's not on its way already), where you can take action and where you might need to put in some work.

You may also have found a new interest in astrology or Tarot. Both would enhance your experience of Qabalah moving forward. Or perhaps a new spiritual technique has shown itself, or a way to enhance your current practices? Remember, they are all to be found on the Tree if you take the time to look.

Whatever you do, get creative, make Qabalah your own. I've seen people use it in their work with crystals, and combine it with their angelic beliefs, but remember you don't need to use any other disciplines or practices, though you might need an interest in human psychology. Which is, of course, inherent in the Tree, too.

I use Qabalah almost every day. I don't sit in meditation or do pathworkings every day, to be clear, but I see Qabalah in my life, I see how the world works, truly works, and I see how I work within it – in it, not of it.

As you do the work, there will be a clearing of your own vision of the reality around you. That can be calming in some ways and frustrating in others. Life is a mix of rain and sunshine, and sometimes you shelter under the Tree for shade, sometimes to keep out of the rain. But it's knowing it's there that's important.

You can find further information on Qabalistic training in the Bibliography and Resources sections.

What I hope you have found is that the Tree comes into your life and is your greatest teacher, not in the form of an individual or even a philosophy or philosophies, but through real-life experience.

The most important thing is to use the tools you now have.

Bibliography

The Archive for Research in Archetypal Symbolism, *The Book of Symbols: Reflections on Archetypal Images*, Taschen, 2010

Kim Arnold, *Tarot: Learn How to Read and Interpret the Cards*, Hay House UK, 2015

Dion Fortune, *The Mystical Qabalah*, Williams and Norgate, 1935

William Gray, *The Ladder of Lights*, Helios, 1968

Julia and Derek Parker, *Parkers' Astrology*, Dorling Kindersley, 1991

Flavia Kate Peters, *Way of the Faery Shaman: The book of spells, incantations, meditations and faery magic*, Moon Books, 2015

Signs and Symbols: An Illustrated Guide to their Origins and Meanings, Dorling Kindersley, 2008

ABOUT THE AUTHOR

David Wells is an outstanding astrologer, past life therapist, author, teacher and presenter whose unique sense of humour and vibrant personality captivates audiences far and wide. With successful television appearances on *Your Stars*, *Jane Goldman Investigates*, *Big Brother*, *Fame Academy*, *RI:SE*, *GMTV*, *Heaven on Earth* and *Most Haunted*, David is a popular household name within the paranormal genre. He is also a columnist with *NOW* and *Fate and Fortune*, and the astrologer for Scotland's *Daily Record* and *Spirit and Destiny* magazine.

David was born in Kelloholm, Scotland. The turning point in his life came in 1992 when he was hospitalized with severe pneumonia. He remembers being aware of walking down a hospital corridor whilst knowing that his physical body was still in a bed on the ward. This led to the pathways of the Tree of Life and his study of Qabalah.

He started by studying astrology to ground his abilities, and searched for meaningful ways to discover more about himself and to fulfil his life purpose through Qabalah.

It has been a long road from catering manager to spiritual teacher, and along the way David has discovered personal strengths and faced many challenges. He now works to help others avoid the same pitfalls and celebrate their uniqueness.

davidwells.co.uk

Hay House Podcasts
Bring Fresh, Free Inspiration Each Week!

Hay House proudly offers a selection of life-changing audio content via our most popular podcasts!

Hay House Meditations Podcast

Features your favorite Hay House authors guiding you through meditations designed to help you relax and rejuvenate. Take their words into your soul and cruise through the week!

Dr. Wayne W. Dyer Podcast

Discover the timeless wisdom of Dr. Wayne W. Dyer, world-renowned spiritual teacher and affectionately known as "the father of motivation." Each week brings some of the best selections from the 10-year span of Dr. Dyer's talk show on Hay House Radio.

Hay House Podcast

Enjoy a selection of insightful and inspiring lectures from Hay House Live events, listen to some of the best moments from previous Hay House Radio episodes, and tune in for exclusive interviews and behind-the-scenes audio segments featuring leading experts in the fields of alternative health, self-development, intuitive medicine, success, and more! Get motivated to live your best life possible by subscribing to the free Hay House Podcast.

Find Hay House podcasts on iTunes, or visit www.HayHouse.com/podcasts for more info.

Listen. Learn. Transform.

Embrace your most sacred life with unlimited Hay House audios!

Live more consciously, strengthen your relationship with the Divine, and cultivate inner peace with world-renowned authors and teachers—all in the palm of your hand. With the *Hay House Unlimited* Audio app, you can learn and grow in a way that fits your lifestyle . . . and your daily schedule.

With your membership, you can:

- Tap into the power of your mind and heart, dive deep into your soul, rise above fear, and draw closer to Spirit.

- Explore thousands of audiobooks, meditations, immersive learning programs, podcasts, and more.

- Access exclusive audios you won't find anywhere else.

- Experience completely unlimited listening. No credits. No limits. No kidding.

Try for FREE!

HAY HOUSE

Look within

Join the conversation about latest products, events, exclusive offers and more.

 Hay House UK

 @HayHouseUK

 @hayhouseuk

 healyourlife.com

We'd love to hear from you!

Printed in the United States
by Baker & Taylor Publisher Services